English
Martial
Arts

Terry Brown

Anglo-Saxon Books

Published 1997 by

Anglo-Saxon Books
Frithgarth
Thetford Forest Park
Hockwold-cum-Wilton
Norfolk
England

Printed by

Redwood Books
Kennet House
Kennet Way
Trowbridge
Wiltshire
England

A Cataloguing-in-Publication record for this book
is available from the British Library.

ISBN 1–898281–18–1

In memory of my parents Lawrence and Eileen Brown, thank you.

To my son Alan.

To the late Sifu 'Uncle' Tan Siew Cheng, Grandmaster of Fong Yang kung fu (The Beggars Art) for guiding me along the martial way and teaching me much about life in the process. If not for him my path would not have led me to this book.

To Robert Pooley for a lifetime of unflagging friendship and support.

ACKNOWLEDGEMENTS

The British Library. The Victoria and Albert Library. The Bodlian Library. The Royal Armouries Library. The Public Records Office. The College of Arms. The Wallace Collection. The Mary Rose Trust. The Dean and Chapter of Durham Cathedral. The Histrionix Living History Group. The Head Librarian and staff at Mill Hill public library, North West London, where the seed of this book first germinated.

I would also like to record my gratitude to the following people: Frank Docherty for his assistance in the photographic shoot for this book. Stephen Pollington for his invaluable and generous assistance in translating archaic texts and his part in the editing of this book. Marcus Tylor for his photography. My publishers Tony and Pearl Linsell for their good humoured patience, faith, advice, and sheer hard work in nurturing this book through its formative stages.

Photographs are supplied by kind permission of the following: the Trustees of The Wallace Collection, London; the Mary Rose Trust; the Dean and Chapter of Durham; the Histrionix Living History Group.

CONTENTS

FOREWORD

The present century has seen an explosion of popularity in the martial arts: kung fu, karate, taekwondo, among others, are names and systems that immediately spring to mind. It is therefore understandable that many in the West regard the Orient as the home, or the Mecca, of martial arts. This means that many of us have tended to accept that European cultures did not have formal martial arts systems, and that when our fighting men (and women) went into battle they did so as members of the 'hack 'em and bash 'em brigade'. It is hoped that this book will prove to its readers that this is far from being the truth. The information given in these pages will make it clear that the English had at their disposal an extremely sophisticated martial arts system that was every bit as effective as those originating in the Orient.

We are fortunate that a large amount of information about English martial arts has survived but it is certain that much more has been lost. The early material was recorded in a small number of manuscripts and books that were vulnerable to the ravages of time, climate and accident. Some information was not recorded simply because it was of no interest to those who had the resources to have manuscripts and books made. There was also deliberate suppression and destruction of knowledge. The Christian Church, for example, actively sought to strengthen its hold on newly converted societies by suppressing such indigenous knowledge as it felt harmful to its cause. There were also heathen vikings who, in their search for wealth, ravaged the very places where written knowledge was likely to be stored. A later instance of wanton destruction is the Dissolution of the Monasteries during the reign of Henry VIII. The great monastic libraries contained secular as well as religious and legal works but all suffered short shrift as a result of Henry's policies. Shiploads of books and manuscripts were sold abroad where they were stripped down and used as bindings and backing sheets in the production of foreign books. A good example of this being the discovery in 1860 of fragments of the Old English poem Waldere written on two sides of a single sheet used in the binding of a book held at the Royal Library in Copenhagen.

Similar acts of vandalism occurred during the Puritan era when Protestant reformers did their best to remove all forms of pleasure from society. They believed that life should be based on pious observance of the scriptures. Sport, secular plays and suchlike were considered to be the work of the devil and so were frowned on. During that period the leaves of 'unsuitable' books were used for, among other things, cleaning materials and toilet paper.

In a sense, the loss of books and manuscripts was of more consequence to later historians than to the warriors of the day. They, after all, were privy to the knowledge and instruction of their contemporaries. What really 'killed off' traditional European martial arts were the rapid advances in military science. After all, traditional fighting skills would have little opportunity for expression when facing a force equipped with cannon and rifles.

As a rule of thumb, the decline of close-quarter fighting arts was inverse to the increasing importance of the science of ballistics in warfare. This decline was first evident in the technically advanced European states and as a result they were the first to 'lose' their traditional close-quarter fighting systems. Under such circumstances we might expect that the military obsolescence of weapons and tactics would have automatically consigned them to evolution's rubbish bin. Life, however, is rarely that absolute and for a variety of reasons many traditional European martial arts survived for a while longer, either to meet the requirements of civilian self-defence or as sports. In the case of the former, the introduction of effective police forces gradually reduced the need for self-defence. In the case of the latter, changing social and moral values created a distaste for the violent, vicious, and bloody gladiatorial combats that were once so popular in England. Those sports that have survived from that time are now so sanitised that they bear little resemblance to the battlefield originals. Many Oriental martial arts systems survived virtually unchanged for longer than the European systems simply because they were the product of nations which, then, lagged behind Europe in science and technology, and as a result still used traditional martial arts on the battlefield.

Moving from the military world to that of documentary evidence the reader will notice what appears, in original manuscripts and quotations, to be some very indifferent spelling. This could be taken as a sign of a poorly educated originator, which indeed may have been the case. However, leaving aside the fact that the ill-educated rarely wrote manuscripts or, as would have it now, books, it must be taken into account that there was not, until comparatively recently, such a thing as standard English. Individuals, even those with a university education, tended to spell according to their accents and dialects, as phonetics played a much more important role in writing than it does now. Dictionaries, as we know them today, simply did not exist. In 1580 William Bullokar in publishing a book for "perfect reading and writing" suggested the need for a dictionary of the English language. However, such dictionaries as followed his plea, for example that of Robert

Cawdrey in 1604, tended to concentrate on the more difficult words. It was not until the eighteenth century, following calls from leading academics, that serious attempts were made to produce wordbooks that, while still not comparable to modern dictionaries, would at least be recognised as such today. It is probable that the first 'modern' style dictionary was the Oxford English Dictionary begun by J. A. Murray in 1879.

One final point to be made concerns the use of battlefield statistics. Judging or estimating the size of bygone armies has never been an easy task and some historians avoid the issue altogether rather than risk errors. In this book the criterion for choosing battle descriptions has been their relevance to the subject matter rather than the figures they quote. A good example of this is the reference to the battle of Flodden (page 71) which is taken from the *History of the British Army* by Fortesque. We are told that the Scots fielded 40,000 men to the 26,000 of the English yet Derek Wilson in his book, *England in the Age of Thomas More* tells us that the Scots only numbered 20,000. Both agree that 10,000 Scots died. The Micropaedia Britanica on the other hand gives 30,000 for the Scots and 20,000 for the English.

In closing this foreword I would like to point out that I have not invented any of the techniques in this book. All of the techniques and methods given are from contemporary sources.

1 BACKGROUND

You are cordially invited to step into the little known world of English martial arts where you will discover a realm of infinite surprises, including professional swordswomen, blind martial arts masters, renegade clergymen, katas, gradings, and even inter-club competitions. Indeed the history, methods, and sheer diversity of English martial arts should be a source of interest and delight to martial artists the world over.

Tracing the history of English martial arts, or indeed that of any ancient system, is not an easy task as fact often fades into supposition and then merges with myth. For the most part it is better to regard such myths as a colourful backdrop to the main story, although some of them do provide a tantalising glimpse of the martial skills of our forebears. For example the story of Thor, or Thunor as the Anglo-Saxons called him, who was charged with the task of protecting Asgard (citadel of the Gods) against the forces of evil. To aid him in this task Thor was armed with a 'magic' war-hammer called Mjollnir which was credited with having the power to return to his hand after being thrown. At first glance this appears to be no more than a picturesque example of heathen belief in the supernatural, yet, on ancient memorial stones, Mjollnir is depicted as having a rope or chain attached to its shaft. This sheds light on the subject because, far from relying on magic, Mjollnir was returned to the hands of its user by rather more practical means and indicates that even in those far off days, martial arts were already highly developed and venerated.

Even without the gods, English martial arts have an impressive history. Unlike some systems they are not the fighting arts of a family or village, but the indigenous and empirical fighting arts of an entire nation. The origins of the system are to be found in the heroic traditions of Anglo-Saxon culture. The warriors produced by this culture were renowned throughout Europe for their skills and ferocity and were only, perhaps, equalled by the Vikings who so frequently contended against them. The ultimate, and somewhat bloody, merging of the rovers of Scandinavia, especially those from Denmark, into the English population introduced additional areas of martial expertise into the English system, an example of this being the two-handed battle-axe which the English, already fond of the equally lethal two-handed bill, adopted with relish. This merging of military skills gave rise to a unique and effective fighting art which had, as its final ingredient, the belligerently defended independent character of the English people.

The sources of information about English martial arts are varied and include sagas, poems, manuscripts, chronicles and books, the latter providing valuable information from the sixteenth century onwards. It is clear from these sources that martial arts have always been held dear by Englishmen, which is not surprising when one considers how frequently during its early history England was raided and invaded. With these facts in mind the passion of the English for martial arts can be seen as a zeal for their freedom and independence, though, like modern martial artists, they were also concerned for their personal safety because, in times past, England suffered levels of social violence that make modern society seem, by comparison, like Utopia. Armed robbery, arson, murder, etc. were committed with dreadful regularity by large bands of outlaws who roamed the countryside terrorizing one and all. However, not all of these gangs were unpopular, William Wither's gang stole corn and gave it free to the needy. Another gang, known as the Brotherhood, which was led by Eustace de Folville and his clergyman brother Richard, earned popular acclaim by kidnapping and murdering corrupt officials. The authorities were largely helpless against these ruthless, but superb, fighters. Indeed, such was the prowess of the Brotherhood that King Edward III granted them a pardon in order that they could fight for him in his war against Scotland, for which service their leader was knighted. Roaming, as they did, through Sherwood Forest there must be a suspicion that their adventures provided some of the material for the now world-famous Robin Hood legend.

However, not all of the crimes were motivated by pecuniary lust, there was a great deal of senseless, and sickening, violent crime such as occurs in present day society. For example, there is the case of Roger Styward who was kicked and punched to death by Simon de Peckham in 1326 for dropping some litter outside the shop of the latter. Contemporary to this was the case of Reginald de Freestone whose skull was fractured by a door-bar wielded by William de Grymesby who was annoyed at being woken by the revels of his victim. Copin le Kyng suffered a similar fate in 1301 when he had been foolish enough to harass a man armed with the formidable quarterstaff. Such incidents were widespread and clearly illustrate the need our ancestors had of self-defence skills. Little wonder then that the average Englishmen went about his business armed, a fact noted by the chronicler Holinshed who, in 1586, wrote the following:

> Seldom shall you see one of my countrymen above eighteen or twenty yeares old to go without a dagger at least at his backe or his side, although they are aged burgesses or magistrates of a citie, who in appearance are

most exempt from brabbling and contention. Our nobilitie weare commonly swords or rapiers with these daggers, as doth everie common serving man that followeth his Lord and master...

Finallie, no man travelleth by the waie without his sword or somesuch weapon except the minister, who commonly weareth none at all unlesse it is a dagger or a hanger at his side.

[Aylward, *English Master of Arms...*]

Holinshed's comments were echoed almost two centuries later by Horace Walpole who wrote to Sir Horace Man in 1752 that:

One is forced to travel, even at noon, as if one was going to battle.

This propensity for bearing arms was also commented on by foreigners; following a visit to England the French ecclesiastic, Stephen Perlin, published notes (Paris 1558) containing the following:

...and it is to be noted, that the servants carry pointed bucklers, even those of bishops and prelates, and the men commonly exercise themselves with the bow. The husbandmen, when they till the ground, leave their bucklers and swords, or sometimes their bows in the corner of the field, so that in this land every body bears arms;...

It is clear in the light of these, and many contemporary, statements that the majority, of Englishmen carried weapons, or had the right to do so. It is also important to accept that this applied to the 'lower' social classes of England because this challenges the popular belief that the common people were a helpless downtrodden section of society. In fact, as far as England was concerned, nothing could be further from the truth. However, this belief is understandable because generations of storytellers, and a good few historians, have failed to teach otherwise. In doing so they have overlooked one of the most potent forces in the development of English society and democracy: the ever present threat of armed insurrection forced authority to show the population a respect and consideration that was rare elsewhere. One might profitably regard this attitude as the forerunner of consensus politics.

Nor must it be imagined that the possession of arms was particularly frowned on. In fact statutes were enacted which insisted that all free men owned weapons, thus proving that English monarchs, at one time, appreciated the value of an armed populace, not only to defend the realm against the threat of invasion but also as a bulwark against domestic challenges to their authority. Such an instance occurred during the reign (1087–1100) of William II who, when faced with baronial dissent, turned for support to his 'brave and honourable English'.

It is clear that the right to bear arms was of mutual benefit to king and commons. However, as has already been intimated, this right had a much greater significance than its military efficacy. It was also instrumental in shaping the Englander's attitude to life. Quite simply, to the pre-suffrage Englishman, the right to bear arms was synonymous with his right to freedom. It was the fact that the working classes possessed both weapons and the skill to use them that was largely responsible for breeding into them the sturdy independence for which they were so renowned. They, and the authorities, knew that as long as they were armed they could, if need be, fight for their rights.

The essence of that attitude was perfectly expressed by Donald Walker, a nineteenth century writer and martial artist who, in 1840, wrote the following:

> I am not a less ardent lover of peace than those who inculcate non-resistance I only differ from them as to the means of ensuring peace. All we have yet seen of men proves that they ever seek to aggrandize themselves at the expense of their neighbours. The individuals of a society are indeed tolerably obedient to the law; but, even in it, when power is given to a particular class, it always robs its neighbours. Governments also find, in the fact that the people have submitted to spoliation, the most conclusive argument that they ought still to submit to it. And as to contiguous states, the feebleness of one constitutes its neighbours right of invasion.
>
> The power of resistance puts an end to spoliation. No man robs another who is equally strong and possesses both arms and art to use them. Still less will a small class think of robbing a vastly greater one thus prepared…

Of course the right to bear arms was of little use without the skill, or as Walker puts it, 'the art' to use them. Martial ability is rarely instinctive. It is usually obtained either in actual combat or through skilled tuition. To that end there had long existed in England a large number of martial arts schools, or *Scholes of Fence* as they were once known. Indeed such was the proliferation of these schools that one author, Roger Ascham, when lamenting the decline of archery was moved to write, in 1545, the following:

> For of fence in everie towne there is not only Maisters to teach it, with his Provostes, Usshers, Scholers and other names of Arte and Schole, but there hath not fayled also which have diligently and well favourably written, and is set oute in printe that everye man may rede it.

We can see, therefore, that in the days of Ascham, a respected scholar, martial arts were a thriving business with a widespread network of well organised schools.

The modus operandi of these schools was determined by a legally constituted ruling body which was also charged with maintaining standards and discipline. This ruling body was run by the maisters of Ascham's sixteenth century observations.

Sad to say, the books referred to by Ascham appear not to have survived the vagaries of time. So, for the most part, we are left with brief, and often incidental, accounts furnished by the likes of Ascham and Sir George Buck. (see p.25) The information provided by such gentlemen, though interesting, is far too brief to provide any real clues to the origin and history of the maisters and their organisation. These origins are therefore always likely to be difficult to ascertain with any degree of confidence, though information is sometimes available from unlikely sources. For example, the *Liber Albus* (Book III) records legislation (c.1180 AD) banning fence schools from the City of London:

> And that nobody may hold school of sword and buckler within the city on pain of imprisonment.

A century later (1285) King Edward I enacted legislation which also aimed to prohibit schools of fence from London:

> Also, Foreasmuch as Fools who delight in Mischief, do learn to fence with Buckler, and thereby are the more encouraged to commit their Follies, it is Provided and enjoined that none shall keep school or teach the Art of Fencing with Buckler, within the City, by Night or by Day, and if any so do, he shall be imprisoned for Forty Days.
>
> [Translation from *Statutes of the Realm*, 1810]

Edward's legislation, bearing in mind his well known penchant for military enterprise, is somewhat paradoxical. It may therefore be that such legislation was at the behest of the civic authorities rather than the king himself.

The existence of such legislation confirms the antiquity of a profession that almost certainly predated it by several generations. It is the author's belief that the maisters, or their martial predecessors, were in existence at least as early as the reign of King Alfred the Great (871–899). Clearly, before a certain point, there is a scarcity of information relevant to the maisters and their profession.

This absence of early documentation is probably due to the fact that in those times the recording of information was an expensive and time consuming business carried out mainly by monks. Their primary concerns were writing down theological works, codes of law, and titles to land. Other matters were of course recorded but it seems reasonable to assume that the activities of individual members of society, such as the maisters of defence, would receive scant attention from those blessed with the gift of penmanship.

Such legislation has not made the researcher's task any easier since there can be little doubt that it encouraged the maisters towards discretion, perhaps even secrecy. The antipathy towards them displayed by contemporary legislation was still evident even during the reign of their great benefactor, Henry VIII (see p.20), when they were able to practice and teach their skills openly, fencing masters were still, strictly speaking, classified as vagrants.

Despite the absence of an obvious lineage for the maisters of defence there are certain professions which may be worth considering when searching for their roots. For example, it is possible that they were descended from military instructors such as those mentioned by the twelfth century Danish chronicler Saxo Grammaticus. Right up to the present day such men have gone on to teach their skills for a living after departing the military. Another possibility is that they evolved from pugils, although the term more properly refers to boxers it does seem that it came to be applied to professional martial artists who hired themselves out as champions (proxy combatants) in trials-by-combat. We know from entries in official documents that such men existed at least as early as the twelfth century, examples of such entries being Wilemus Pugilus (1156) and Laurencius Pugil (1176). Indeed this was still the case three centuries later (1571) as we know from an account given in Holinshed's Chronicles of a dispute over land and other property. The issue was to be decided in trial-by-combat between champions representing plaintiff and appellant. One of the champions, George Thorne, is described as, "a bigge, broad, strong set fellow". The other contestant was Henry Nailor, who was specifically described as a master of defence. Nailor, who was in the employ of the Earl of Leicester, is mentioned in the official records of the Company of Maisters, where he is listed as a maister as early as 1568.

As for the ruling body which regulated the affairs of the maisters it appeared to operate along lines not entirely dissimilar to those of the merchant guilds with which it was contemporaneous. As evidence of this, albeit partial, we can consider a piece of legislation contained in the *Liber Albus* which treats of apprenticeships. The legislation in question states that the master and his apprentice(s) should go to the Guildhall and agree the covenant and terms with four reputable men of the trade. The 'four reputable men' would seem to be the counterparts of the 'Four Ancient Maisters' (see p.25) who supervised the Company of Maisters.

Regardless of supposition about the origin of the maisters or their organisation it is evident that it is human nature for individuals to endeavour to pass on their skills to the next generation. This can be on a one-to-one basis, as in father to son or mother to daughter, or, when commercial or military requirements dictate, from an individual to a group. Therefore, the origins of the maisters and their ruling body are of less importance than their purpose, which was to teach and maintain martial arts to a high standard and, in addition, to protect and propagate their own interests. We may therefore reasonably suppose that they were responding to the same social and business trends that led to the creation of other guilds.[1]

Regardless of their origins the maisters, individually and corporately, managed to survive the social and legislative pressures ranged against them. Not that this should come as a surprise because, quite apart from the toughness which was a pre-requisite of their livelihood, it is also clear that the distaste with which the maisters were viewed by the civic authorities was not necessarily shared by others. Even the occasional regal attacks against their profession were more than balanced by frequent examples of monarchical support. For example, in 1446 Philip Treher, presumably a maister of defence, was appointed by King Henry VI to teach the art of arms to a young apprentice called John Davy who was to undergo trial-by-combat against his employer, William Catour, whom he had accused of treason. This situation was immortalised by William Shakespeare in his play, *Henry VI* (Act II. Scene III.), though he renamed Catour as Horner, and Davy as Peter Thump. Treher was obviously a good tutor because his young pupil was victorious.

In the wake of such august support it was clearly only a matter of time before the maisters received legal recognition. This came in the form of a 'Royal Warrant' issued by King Henry VIII directing his Lord Chancellor to pass Letters Patent under the authority of the Great Seal. This patent not only granted the maisters legal recognition it also effectively granted them the monopoly for teaching martial arts in England. In effect, Henry created a martial arts commission, or ruling body, for English martial arts. This organisation had stronger powers than its present day equivalent, as will be seen from the wording of the document:

> Ric. Beste, Humph. Basset, Rob. Polmorth, John Legge, Peter Beste, Philip Williams, Ric. Lord, John Vincent, Nic. de la Haye, masters of the 'Science of Defence,' and Will. Hunt, John Frye, Hen. Whytehead, Gilbert Bekett Edw. Pynner, Thos. Tourner, Jeffrey Gryffyn, Thos. Hudson, Thos. Tymsey, Hen. Thyklyppes and John ap Ryce, provosts of the said science. Commission to enquire and search, in all parts of England, Wales, and Ireland for persons being scholars of the said science of defence (many of whom, regardless of their oaths made to their masters on first entering to learn the said science, upon the cross of a sword in remembrance of the Cross whereon Our Lord suffered, have for their own lucre of their 'unsaciable covetous minds,' without sufficient licence, resorted to all parts of England, keeping open schools and taking great sums of money for their labours, and yet have insufficiently instructed their scholars, to the

---

[1] The earliest known English guild was the ninth century CNIHTAS guild of Canterbury.

great slander of the masters and provosts of the science and of the good and laudable orders and rules of the same), and to take any scholar so misusing himself before the nearest justice of the peace to be bound in sufficient sureties not to repeat his offences against his said oath and the said orders and rules, or in case of refusal to be committed to goal.

[West., 20 July. 32 Hen. VIII. Del. Westm. 20 July S.B.]

Henry's warrant was a tremendous fillip for English martial arts and its teachers because it not only made their survival easier, it also guaranteed, as far as was humanly possible, that set standards of excellence would be maintained; which is of course one of the aims of present-day governing bodies. If that had been all that Henry had done it would have been more than enough to have earned him the eternal gratitude of the maisters. In the event he was to do far more, because on several occasions he attended their prizes (gradings) and their challenges (competitions). This added respectability to legality, because anything that met with the monarch's approval must, *ipso facto*, be respectable. Henry's patronage was to have a beneficial secondary effect, because his enthusiastic support of the maisters was to provide them with effective protection against the machinations of their erstwhile enemies, London's civic rulers, who, for the most part, were forced to hold their peace.

The patent granted by Henry VIII was not to last for long, because, as was the custom, it lapsed upon his death in 1547. It was to be nearly sixty years before the maisters were again to enjoy such legal status. For, despite the claims of the maisters, it would seem that none of Henry's children renewed the Patent when they succeeded to the throne. Nonetheless, such was the standing and popularity of the maisters that the said monarchs, Edward VI, Mary I, and Elizabeth I, all attended prizes and challenges. Despite this recognition the English maisters of defence owed thanks to a Scottish monarch for the full restoration of the legal rights granted to them by Henry VIII. It was James VI of Scotland who, as James I of England, granted the maisters, in 1605, a warrant which renewed the powers that they had held in the mid-sixteenth century. James also, like his predecessors, gave the maisters social respectability by twice commanding them to give demonstrations for his entertainment.

It might be thought that the legal and social accolades which James I afforded the maisters would lead to further growth and prosperity but they turned out to be the final high notes in a totally unexpected swan-song. In just twenty-five years this once powerful and popular organisation ceased, as far as is known, to exist. We may never know the reasons for its demise though there are several factors which may have played a part in its disastrous change of fortunes. For example, in 1623, Parliament approved the *Monopolies Act*. This legislation had the laudable purpose of preventing political and commercial corruption but, unfortunately, it also had an adverse effect upon legitimate and beneficial monopolies, such as that enjoyed by the maisters of defence.

Then, in 1630, the maisters suffered a further set-back when the Privy Council were prevailed upon to ban certain public gatherings from taking place. This effectively prevented the maisters from holding their prizes and challenges, and was a much more serious blow than may at first glance be realised. Prizes and challenges were held in public so that the world could see that they were conducted honestly but they also served the purpose of raising funds and recruiting new students. The ban may, therefore, have led to a decline in the Organisation's membership. It also seems to indicate that the maisters had lost the safety-net of royal patronage and this would not be surprising as the monarch of the day was Charles I. He was no doubt too busy devising the schemes which were to visit war and devastation upon his country to consider overmuch the interests of those affected by the Privy Council ruling. It should be pointed out that the maisters were not the only ones to suffer from the ruling of 1630, it also banned, for example, theatrical performances. The reason given for the Privy Council ban was that large gatherings of people would encourage the spread of the plague.

Finally, when considering the demise of the maisters, it is perhaps worth taking into account changing social attitudes, albeit temporary changes. There was abroad at that time a puritanical approach to life which had been gathering momentum since Elizabethan times. Puritanical zeal reached its peak in 1644 when Parliament enacted a law aimed against various kinds of entertainment. This new philosophy may well have had a greater effect on the maisters than any amount of legislation. Be that as it may, the last known reference to the Company of Maisters was made in an appendix, written by Sir George Buck, that was included in the 1631 edition of Stow's *Annales*.

> The art Gladiatorie which wee call the Science of Defence (and the Italians Scrimia & arte del arme)... In this city [London] there bee many professors thereof, and very skilful men in teaching the best and most offensive and defensive use of very many Weapons, as of the long sword, the backe sword, the Rapier and dagger, the single Rapier, the case of Rapiers, the sword and buckler or targate, the Pike, the Holberd, the long staffe, and other, King Henry the 8. made the professors of this Art a company or corporation by Letters Patents, wherein the Art is intituled the noble Science of Defence. Of this Art Gladiatorie there be divers Schooles in London kept by the Masters of Defence: . . . The manner of the proceedings of our fencers in their Schooles, is this: first they which desire to be taught, at their admission are called Schollers, and as they profit, they take degrees, and that must be

wonne by publique tryall of their proficiency, and of their skill at certaine weapons, which they call prizes, and in the presence and view of many hundreds of people. And at their next and last prize, well and sufficiently performed, they doe proceed Masters of the Science of Defence or Masters of fence, as wee commonly call them. The King ordained that none but such as have thus orderly proceeded by publique act and triall, and have the approbation of the principall Masters of their company, may professe or teach this Art of Defence publikely in any part of England...

Whatever the causes of their demise, the maisters of defence, like the old soldiers of proverbial fame, didn't die, they just faded away. However, before they faded away they were to take part in the next great phase of English martial arts. Indeed they were probably instrumental in its birth.

In the second half of the seventeenth century Samuel Pepys made some invaluable entries in his now famous diaries. One of those entries recorded details of his first ever visit to the playing of a prize. At first it might appear that he was indicating the survival of the traditional prizing or grading of the old style maisters but closer examination will show that while he, and others, were using the term prize, what they were actually witnessing was a version of the challenge or competition. There was though one crucial difference. Unlike their predecessors (who trained with blunted weapons) this new breed of martial artists, or stage-gladiators as they were called, fought with unrebated weapons.

In a moral, or philosophical sense this development can only be viewed with a certain amount of regret, in that it represented an abandonment of long held principles. Equally important is the fact that the use of lethal weapons led to the modification and forsaking of many of the traditional fighting techniques of the maisters. This was an understandable development which was intended to prevent deaths, if not serious injuries. Certainly there is a parallel in modern times where many dangerous techniques are outlawed from martial arts tournaments. However, it did mean that many effective, battle-proven techniques fell into disuse, while other conventional methods, such as the drawing cut, gained a disproportionate value in the stage-gladiator's repertoire.

In their planned intention of preventing fatalities the gladiators were largely successful, though there was a price to be paid. The English public, long used to the military fierceness which typified traditional English martial arts, were a little suspicious of this new, more cautious, style of fighting. This led, on occasions, to the belief that some of the new style contests were fixed. It would of course be foolish to think, knowing human nature, that such things never happened. However, on balance, this seems a rather unfair judgement because the records show that most such contests were fought in genuine earnest with many painful wounds given and received.

The recollections of Samuel Pepys show that he had initially been one of the doubters:

June 1st 1663

…walked to the New Theatre, which, since the King's players are gone to the Royal one, is this day begun to be employed by the fencers to play prizes at. And here I came and saw the first prize I ever saw in my life: and it was between one Matthews, who did beat at all weapons, and one Westwicke, who was soundly cut several times both in the head and legs, that he was all over blood: and other deadly blows did they give and take in earnest, till Westwicke was in a most sad pickle. They fought at eight weapons, three bouts at each weapon. It was well worth seeing, because I did till this day think that it had only been a cheat: but this being upon a private quarrel, they did it in good earnest: and I felt one of their swords, and found it to be very little, if at all blunter on the edge, than the common swords are. Strange to see what a deal of money is flung to them both upon the stage between every bout…

The observation that the fight was 'upon a private quarrel' could, by inference, cause one to doubt that non-grudge fights were equally well contested but later writers, including those from overseas, tend to support Pepys's new found conviction in the integrity of effort displayed by the stage-gladiators. Further entries in his diaries should remove any doubt about this from the mind of the reader:

September 9th 1667

…After dinner, he and I and my wife to the Bear-Garden, to see a prize fought there. …I stood and saw the prize fought, till one of them, a shoemaker, was so cut in both his wrists that he could not fight any longer, and then they broke off: his enemy was a butcher. The sport very good…

Pepys returns to the theme nearly two years later:

April 12th 1669

…thence by water to the Bear-Garden, …Here we saw a prize fought between a soldier and a country fellow, one Warrell, who promised the least in his looks, and performed the most of valour in his boldness and evenness of mind, and smiles in all he did, that I ever saw: and we were all both deceived and infinitely taken with him. He did soundly beat the soldier, and cut him over the head. Thence back to White Hall, mightily pleased, all of us, with this sight, and particularly this fellow, as a most extraordinary man for his temper and evenness in fighting.

There can be no good reason to doubt the diarist's observations. Nonetheless, there can be little harm in considering the views of other writers. Monsieur Cesar de Saussure, of Lausanne, Switzerland, wrote to his family giving an account of English gladiatorial combats. His words are particularly interesting because they prove the existence of female gladiators. In 1720 he witnessed a fight between two swordswomen. He records that one of the women was thrown shillings and half-crowns when she inflicted a serious cut to her opponent's forehead. The victim's wound was sewn up and, after stiffening her resolve with a large glass of spirits, she returned to the fray. She quickly received another wound, this too was sewn up on stage during which time her opponent was again rewarded with coins. The twice-wounded woman bravely rejoined the fray only to receive a third wound, this time right across the neck and throat. This injury was so bad that she was unable to continue the fight. Our chronicler records that the women fought with three kinds of weapon. The two hand sword, sword and dagger, and finally sword and shield. An interesting observation to be made about such contests, apart from the courage of the combatants, is the extraordinary repose and good humour that was invariably displayed, and commented on by observers. In these qualities our two ladies were as blessed as any male gladiator as de Saussure shows with the following observations:

> As soon as they appeared on the stage they made the spectators a profound reverence: they then saluted each other and engaged in a lively and amusing conversation. They boasted that they had a great amount of courage, strength, and intrepidity. One of them regretted she was not born a man, else she would have made her fortune by her powers: the other declared she beat her husband every morning to keep her hand in...

Note: It is of interest to consider three points that are raised by the comments of Pepys and Cesar de Saussure. First, the 'prizes', which in days of old were usually held in pub yards or theatres hired for the occasion, were now such big business that they warranted their own regular venue: Second, the gladiators fought with such a large variety of weapons, in this at least they were maintaining the traditions of their predecessors: And finally one sees that the ancient tradition of throwing appreciation money to the fighters had survived, indeed still survives today in modern boxing, where such gifts are known as 'nobbins'.

2 ORGANIZATION

This chapter will, for the most part, be based upon the procedures of an organisation that is known to have governed English martial arts during the sixteenth and seventeenth centuries. The choice of this organisation as an example of martial arts administration is mandatory rather than arbitrary due to the fact that it is the only such organisation about which we have any real knowledge. Indeed it is indicative of the problems of researching this subject that we cannot even be certain as to its correct title. In his warrant of 1540 King Henry VIII appointed the 'Masters of the Science of Defence' as a Commission (of enquiry) without actually naming their organisation. King James I, in his warrant of 1605, charged the 'Masters of ye Noble Science of Defence' with the same duties as those of the Warrant of 1540. Unfortunately he too failed to name their organisation.

However, Sir George Buck, who was Master of the Office of Revels to King James I as well as being a member of the King's Privy Chamber, tells us that:

> …King Henry the 8. made the professors of this Art a company or corporation by Letters Patents… The Armes of this corporation be Gules, a sword Argent pendant.

Although no concrete evidence has, to date, been unearthed proving that the maisters were members of a legally constituted company, the evidence of the warrants of 1540 and 1605 seems to strongly suggest that such was indeed the case. This supposition is, as we have seen, supported by the statement of Sir George Buck. Other incidental, but factual evidence lends support to the theory as, for example, when in July 1582, following complaints from Ambrose, Earl of Warwick, the Lord Mayor of London granted permission for the Earl's servant, John David, to march through the streets of the city with, *his companie drumes and shewe*, on the way to play his provosts prize. Official or not, there can be little doubt that the maisters operated their organisation along lines that were broadly similar to the Companies of the day.

The Company of Maisters appears to have been controlled, or at least supervised by four men known as the 'Four Anciant Maisters'. An anciant, or elder maister was quite simply a person who had seniority over the person who so addressed him. In this the English used the same system found in Chinese martial arts which make use of such terms as younger brother and elder brother.

It is not clear whether the Four Anciant Maisters held absolute authority over the membership or operated as a type of steering committee. The Liber Albus contains legislation that, if applied to the Company of Maisters, would seem to grant the Four Ancient Maisters total authority:

> Of the Penalty for rebelling against the Maisters of the Mysteries
>
> ...And in each mystery there shall be chosen and sworn four or six, or more or less, according as the mystery shall need; which persons, so chosen and sworn, shall have full power from the Mayor well and lawfully to do and to perform the same.
>
> And if any person of the said mysteries shall be rebellious, contradictory, or fractious, that so such persons may not duly, perform their duties, and shall thereof be attainted, he shall remain in prison, the first time, ten days, and shall pay unto the Commonalty ten shillings for such contempt;...

On the other hand there is at least one entry, concerning a disciplinary code, that seems to indicate that the 'ordinary' maisters also had the power to formulate policy. Such entries would seem to indicate some kind of democracy, though on balance one tends to imagine that the Four Ancient Maisters remained the ultimate authority, a situation that would accord very closely to that in modern martial arts associations where masters and chief instructors are not usually renowned for their power sharing.

There were a total of four grades in English martial arts. In ascending order these were: scholler, free scholler, provost, and maister. The rank of anciant maister is best regarded as a courtesy title because it was a way of acknowledging seniority within the organisation. Though it must be added that the Four Ancient Maisters were always referred to as an authoritative unit.

Like any modern day organisation the Company of Maisters had both rules and constitution to govern its mode of operation:

> "The ruills and constitucons of the schole
>
> "OUR soveraigne Lady Elizabeth by the grace of god Quene of Englande ffranc and Irelande Defendor of the faithe and supreme hed (vnder God) of the church of Englande and Irelande &c of her moste ryall and abowndant grace hath licensed every maister and Provost being Englishe men as well within this realme of Englande Irelande and Calleis and the

precincts of the same to kepe and teache in their scholes all manner of estats gentilmen ore yomen of what estate so ever he or they be wch ar willinge to learne the noble sciense of defense as playing wth the two hande sworde, the pike, the bastarde sworde, the dagger, the Backe sworde, the sworde and Buckeler, and the staffe, and all other manner of weapons apperteyninge to the same scienc/ yf their be anny of them willinge to learne the same sciense To thentent that they and every of them beinge schollers of this present schole may knowe the ruills constitutions and ordenancies thearof I Willyam Mucklowe beinge one of the maisters of the same scienc proved and alowed accordinge to order caused this present table to be written That they may soe heare and reade the same ruills constitucons and ordinanceis of this present schole in mañer & forme as hereafter folleth FIRSTE every scholler of what estate or degree soever he or they be shalbe at an agreement with the saide maister or his Deputye of and for soch weapon or weapons as the same scholler or schollers shall be willinge to learne And that donne the same scholler or schollers shall sweare by the crosse of his sworde or weapon wch crosse signifieth and betokeneth the cross which our Saviour Jesus Christe suffered his death upon/ and for the gevinge of his othe he must pay xij^d vnto his maister and for his entrance iiij^d And the same scholler shall pay for his learninge accordinge as his maister and he canne agree And for what soever that he doth agre the sayde scholler shall pay in hande the one halfe/ that is to say, yf he make his bargayne for xl^s then he must pay in hande xx^s/ yf he make his bargayne for xxx^s then he muste pay in hande xv^s and so as the maister and the scholler doth agree/ to paye the one halfe in hande and the other when he is taken out of his quarters And also the same scholler muste bringe his weapons/ or ells to agree wth his maister or his maisters Deputye for them."

The Company of Maisters appears to have been self-regulatory and self-disciplining. Though, when the warrants of Henry VIII and James I were in force, the maisters also had the legal right to march perpetrators of certain offences to the nearest magistrate for judicial chastisement. However, this punitive action would not normally have been applied to their own members. Instead they would have relied on the imposition of fines, weight being added to the persuasiveness of this punishment by barring the guilty party from certain benefits until the fine had been paid:

"It is Agreed gennerally by & betweene every of vs the saide m^{rs} of the noble Science of Defence eche to the other, That if any one or twoe or more of vs doe breake any of the Orders and Constitutions whatsoever belonging to o^r Scyence, That then he or they of vs or any of vs so offending shall be fyned by the rest of vs the saide m^rs as in o^r discrecōns according to the breache shall fyne him or them, And he or they so being fyned not to sit in Judgem^t till the saide fyne & e ūy pte thereof be satisfied or payed, neither he or they shall recyve any dutyes wch belongh to a m^r till the same be payed as aforesaid."

Even the Four Anciant Maisters themselves followed this creed of self-discipline as can be seen from the following agreement made in the year 1550:

"Hear followeth an Indenture of covenants made betwen the four anciant maisters of the noble scienc of Defenc within the Citye of London.

"THIS INDENTURE made the last daye of October In the Therd yeare of the raigne of our soveraigne Lorde Kinge Edward the sixte by the grace of God &c Be twene Willyam Hunt on the one partye, R.G. on the second partie and WB. on the therd partie beinge ancient maisters of the noble scienc of Defence With in the citie of London WITNESETH that the sayde parties have Covenanted condiscended and agreed together in manner and forme the followinge That is to saye every of the same pties covenanteth and grantith to and with the other parties that neither of the saide parties shall from henceforth set forth anny of theire schollers prizes without the consent and agrement of all the sayd parties AND allso that none of their schollers shall play his provosts priz within Vij years after his schollers priz ALLSO the saide parties do likewyese convenaunte and graunte everye of them with the other that none of them shall permitt or suffer anny of their saide schollers after he hath played his Provosts priz, to playe their maisters priz within five yeares after their Provosts priz MOREOUER the same parties ar consented and agreed together That everye of them shall kepe one Boxe whearin they shall put for every scholler that he hath (or from hence forth shall have) ij^d towards the mayntenance of necessaries belonginge to the saide science AND every of them shall kepe a Juste and true boke of the monye in the sayde boxes severally And every of the same parties shall bringe att two sundry tymes in the yeare, all the monye in theire severall boxes gathered, To soch a place as the same maister ∗∗∗∗ [manuscript ends at this point]

The following document, apart from explaining how costs were to be met also gives an insight into the body of rules governing the conduct of challengers:

"Yf ANNY PROVOST doth dwell within twentye myles of the Citye of London wheare all prizes oughte to be playd, then he oughte to beare his owne costs and Charges but if he Dwell more than Twentye myles distant from London Then the Prizor oughte to beare the one halfe of his Charges And so oughte everye maister in like manner at a maisters Prize/ALLSO EUERY maister oughte to be thear to play with the prizor, excepte onely his owne maister whome he playeth vnder/ every provost and freescholler oughte to be thear to make rome as they shall be apoyncted by the maisters/ And the youngest maister oughte to begine firste/ and so in order/ And at anny priz Whether it be maisters priz Provosts prize or freschollers priz who soever dothe play agaynste ye prizor, and doth strike his blowe and close withall so that the prizor cannot strike his blow after agayne, shall wynn no game for any veneye so geven although it shold breake the Prizors head.

GOD SAVE THE QUEEN

Another function of the Company of Maisters was the issuing of teaching licences, known as letters, to students who had successfully prized at the necessary grade. This is a duty fulfilled by most modern day martial arts associations. However, as will be seen, the form of the original licences, and the rhetoric contained in them, were altogether more grandiose than their latter day equivalents:

"A Provosts Letter.

"BE IT KNOWNE vnto all manner of officers vnder the Dominions of our soveraigne Ladye Elizabeth by the grace of God of England ffranc and Ireland Quene Defendor of the faith &c// as Justices of peace maiors sheriffs Bailiffs Cunstables Hedborowes and other her ma^ts lovinge subiects Certifieng you by this lee That it pleaseth our saide moste dreade soveraigne Lady the quenes ma^tie wth her moste honorable privie Counsel to admitt wth authoritie and by especiall commission vnder her highnes greate Seale to geve licenc to vs maisters of defence playinge wth all manner of weapons vsuall to admit and allowe all soch maisters and Provosts to instruct and teach and have experience and counninge sufficient by profe and triall and before vs the saide maisters of the same scienc or the mste of vs openly wth warninge geven to all schollers by bills set vp within the citie of London fourtene dayes and then playinge their prizes wth so many schollers as will playe that daye/ and after that prize so Discharged to challenge for his Provosts prize by bills set vp xxj dayes, all Provosts And so to abide the triall of so many Provosts as will also play that daye Thus doinge openly within the citie of London before vs the ancient maisters of the saide scienc with all other Duetyes wch to a Provost do belonge THEN we, Richarde

White Thomas Weaver, Willyam Hearne, Willyam Glover als Thompson, Willyam Joyner, Henry Naylor, Richard Donne and Edmond Darcye being all maisters of the same science dwellinge w^(th)in the citie of London Do admitt Willyam Mucklowe as a Provost vnder Thomas Weaver of our saide scienc the iiij day of Juyne in the yeare of our Lorde God 1568 in the x^(th) yeare of the raigne of our soveraigne Ladie the Quenes Ma^(tie) for as much as the saide Willyam Mucklowe did play his Provosts priz within the Citie of London the day and yeare above written And before vs the maisters of the said scienc We thearfore do by theis p̄nts admitt the saide Will͞m Mucklow to instructe and teach w^(th)in the Quenes ma^(tis) Dominions as an hable and well tried man with diverse weapons as, the longesworde, the backsworde the rapier and dagger and the staffe AND thearfor we beinge maisters admitted by the Quenes moste excellent Mat^(ie) and her honorable Counsell as aforesaide, do praye and desyer all her highnes officers and true subiects to ayde the saide Willyam Mucklow agaynst all strayngers and soch as take vppon them to teach without authoritie wilfully forswearinge them selves/ w^(ch) have a longe tyme deceaved her Ma^(ts) lovinge subiects Whearfore we the saide maisters Thomas Weaver, Willyam Hearne, Will͞m Glover, Will͞m Joyner, Henry Naylor, Richard Donne and Edmond Darcye. desyer all her highnes officers as they love God and our soveraigne Ladye the queenes Ma^(tie) to suffer none to teach or kepe anny schole of Defence whatsoever he or they be excepte he or they have authoritie to shew in like case as this Provost hath Thus doinge you shall shewe your selfes true and faythfull subiects and officers vnto our moste dreade soveraigne Lady the Quenes Ma^(tie) Thankes be geven to God for maynteyninge of the truethe IN WITNES Whearof &c."

The granting of a teaching licence was the ultimate proof of ability and rank but it was by no means the only ceremony to the recognition of promotion. Another equally important procedure to be observed for the successful prizor was the swearing of an oath which reflected the responsibilities attendant on the student's new rank. Unfortunately the author has not been able to unearth all of the oathes that were employed. Though there are tantalizing references to them in the provosts' oath itself.

The oath, be it maister's or provost's, was much more than the mere act of swearing allegiance to one's organisation. It was in fact an all-encompassing code of behaviour which the swearer was expected to live by. It reflected the ambient attitude of the Englander to politics, philosophy, religion, and morality. The newly promoted provost would have sworn his obligations in the following manner:

"The Provosts Othe

"1. INP'MIS YOU shall sweare so helpe you God and halidome and by the christendome wch god gave you at the fount stone and by the Crosse of this sworde whiche dothe represent vnto you the crosse wch our saviour Jesus Christe did suffer his moste paynefull deathe and passion vpon for our redemption/ That you shall vpholde mayntayne and kepe to you^r power all soch articles as shalbe declared vnto you by me beinge your maister in the presenc of theis my bretheren and maisters hear/ wch you intend to procede vnto.

"2. ITEM you shall be true to the Catholike churche to augment and farther the true faythe of God to your power as all true Christians ought to do.

"3. ITEM you shalbe true subiect tour soveraigne Ladye Quene Elizabethe and to her successors kings of this realme of Englande and not to knowe of anny treason but that you vtter it wth in four and twentie howers at the farthest, & soner yf you canne and to serve her and hers agaynst all nations to the vttermost of your power.

"4. ITEM you shalbe true provoste from this daye vnto the last daye of your life to love and serve the trueth and hate falshode, never to rebell or go agaynste anny m^r or provost of this scienc, as all provosts ought to be ruelled by their owne maister and the rest of the maisters his bretheren, as other Provosts have donne heartofore, accordinge to the ancient orders of our scienc.

"5. ITEM You shall sweare not to teache anny suspecte person as a murtherer, a thefe, a common drunkarde or soch as be common quarellers but to avoyde your hands of them, and to kepe no companye with them so nigh as you canne.

"6. ITEM you shall not teache anny person whatsoever he or thcy be without you do sweare him with soche alike oathe as your maister and other maisters my bretheren shall assigne you and no other othe but the verye same.

"7. ITEM you shall not challenge anny m^r or compare with anny m^r as to disprayese his doings/ and especially you shall not compare with me your maister/ vnder whome you do now procede/and of whome you have had your Cunninge/ nether in Challenge or with approbrius words as touchinge our scienc in anny wyes.

"8. ITEM that at anny priz or game which you shalbe at ether to stick or to stande by you shall say the truethe of that wch you shall see when you be asked or called to speake, and not ells yf there be anny maister in place, or anny pvost being your elder and ancient/ And when you shalbe so asked or demaunded you shall geve true Judgement of that which you have seene so nighe as you canne, settinge all affections aparte and rightely to Judge without fraud or guyle even as you woulde be Judged of God/ helpinge them to that wch they have wone so nighe as you canne or maye by your good will.

"9. ITEM you shalbe alwayes mercifull and whearas it maye happen you to have the vpper hande of your enimye That is to saye vnder your feete or without weapon or some other advantage you shall not kill him, yf he be the Queenes true subiect, savinge your selfe without danger of deathe or bodeley hurte accordinge to your first othe wch you Received entringe to learne the scienc.

"10. ITEM you shall not make anny vsher without the licenc of your maister, but for neade you may have a deputie/ wch shall not geve anny other othe but this That is to saye/ yf you be absent he may take in such as wilbe schollers sayinge to them thus/ You shall sweare so help you God and holydome and by the crosse of this sworde that you shalbe content to receave such an othe as my m^r or his pvost shall geve vnto you at your next metinge together/ And so to take him scholler and geve him his first lesson.

"11. ITEM you shall not entice or trayne anny other maisters scholler to teache or cause him to be taughte without the goodwill of his first maister Excepte the sayd scholler have well and truelye contented and payde his fore saide maister his full duetye And furthermore you shall kepe or cause to be kepte our orders ruills and constitutions in all prizes as we have partely/ declared vnto you/ and shall more at large hearafter as you shall farther procede in the scienc of defence.

"12. ITEM you shall sweare to kepe this Provosts othe in all poyncts nowe geven and declared vnto you by me beinge your maister in the precense of theis my bretheren/ and maisters of this scienc so help you God and holydome."

The twelve items of the provosts' oath give a clear indication of the importance that the Company of Maisters placed upon the duties of the Provost. As was to be expected, the maisters oath was even more demanding than that for provosts, and from item three onwards it clearly demonstrates the extra moral and social responsibilities that fell upon the holder of the higher rank.

The Maisters Othe.

1. FFIRST you shall sweare so helpe you god and halidome and by all the christendome which God gave you at the fount stone and by the Crosse of this sworde which doth represent vnto you the Crosse wch our saviour Jesus Christe suffered his most paynefull death uppon, That you shall vpholde maynteyne and kepe to your power all soch articles as shalbe heare declared vnto you and receved in the presenc of me your maister and theise the reste of the maisters my bretheren beinge psent hear with me at this tyme.

2. ITEM you shalbe true to the Catholicke churche to augment and further the true faythe of Christe to your power as all true xpians oughte to do of righte.

3. ITEM you shalbe true subiect to our soveraigne Ladye quene Elizabethe and to her successors Kings of this relme of England And not to know of anny pson or persons committinge anny treason although it weare your owne father but that you vtter it within xxiiij howers or soner yf you canne/ or yf it lye in your power/ And alwayes to be ready to Spende bothe your lyfe and your goodes In the Sarvis of the quens majestye wher she shall Command yowe at all tymes agaynst her Enymyes/

4. ITEM you shalbe true maister from this daye forward to the laste daye of your life, loving trueth, hating falcehod and not grudginge or disdeyninge anny maister of this scienc when you or anny of vs you shall not breake the ancient orders Excepte it be donne by the Consent of thre of the maisters for the better orderinge of our scienc And you alwayes to be rueled by your bretheren beinge maisters of this scienc, and especially yf anny maister be in place wch is your ancient or elder.

5. ITEM you shall not teache anny suspecte person, as a murtherer a thefe a common Drunkearde nor soch as you knowe to be common quarellers/ nor to kepe company with them But to avoyde all soch so nighe as you canne A maisterlesse man you shall not maynteyne or succour within your schole yf you may knowe of him.

6. ITEM yf it chance that you come to anny manner of priz or game or anny kynde of play at weapons touchinge our science, you shall without respect favor or hatred of either partye, saye speake and geve true Judgement of that which you shall se theare Even as you would be Judged your selfe wth out respecte of either partye Declaringe the trueth and right so nigh as you can or maye.

7.   ITEM you shall take in no scholler to thentente to teache him or cause him to be taughte anny manner of weapon or weapons apperteyninge to the scienc except you geve him his right oth which belongeth to a scholar And to take for his learninge as other maisters do vse to take, not to take lesse the other maisters do, to spyte or to hinder any other maister of this scienc but to do as you woulde be donne to.

8.   ITEM you ought not to challenge anny maister within this realme of Englande beinge an Englisheman/ And especially you shall not challenge you^r maister of whome you had your counninge and vnder whome you do procede and ar made maister AND farther vppon your maisters othe you shall well and truelye contente and paye yor maister for all soche manner of debts duetyes and demaunds which be dew betwyxte your maister and you And him to love and honor as your maister and your Ancient.

9.   ITEM you shalbe mercifull, And whearas you happen to have the vpper hande of your enimye That is to saie wth out weapon or vnder your feete or his backe towards you then you shall not kill him savinge yourselfe harmlesse without daunger of death Excepte it bein the service of the prince: And also yf you heare of anny varyance betwyxt m^r & m^r / or m^r and pvost, or pvost and pvost or free scholler and free scholler you shall do the beste yt you can to make them frends And alwayes to kepe the peace yf you can.

10.   ITEM you shall ayde and strengthen to your power (yf you see them wrongede) and helpe all maisters and Provosts of this scienc, all widdowes and fatherless childeren/ And yf you knowe anny maister of scienc that is fallen into sicknes being in povertye you shall put the maisters in rememberance at all prizes and games and other assemblies that they may se him to have duetye and to hav him in rememberanc the soner for your good worde/ Even as other shall do for you yf the cause weare a like.

11.   ITEM you shall not sett forthe anny prize nor to kepe but one skolle in London within twelve moneths and a daye after the playinge of your maisters prize, nor teache or cause to be taughte anny other maisters scholler excepte you have the goodwill of his firste maister, without the saide scholler hath payde his first maister all his duetye for his learninge.

12.   ITEM you shall at no tyme set forwarde anny manner of provst or free schollers priz but that you firste calle the maisters together requieringe thear goodwills in that behalfe And with the consents of them havinge

their goodwills to geve lawfull warnng as you shalbe instructed by the assents/ wheare it shalbe playde, and what daye is appoyncted.

13. ITEM you shall not for lucar sake set forwards anny priz of a m^r provost or free scholler wthout a lawful cause of him or them had and taken by you and at the leste ij maisters more besydes you^r selfe, for vnto that you ar sworne And at anny prizes set forwarde by you and the consents of the maisters, you to see that everye maister and provost have his duetye wch he oughte to have in the place for the prizes beinge accordinge to our ancient orders and ruills.

14. ITEM you shall not promisse any person learninge, but that you do teach him or cause him to be taughte as a maister ought of right to do That is to saye, a scholler like a scholler a Provost like a Provost and a maister like a maister to the vttermost of your power Entringe in his degrees without hidinge from them that which belongethe to them of right Recevinge their othe and kepinge it truelye, soch ought to be taughte the effecte of our science, savinge the same which shall kepe the scienc out of Slander.

15. ITEM you shall not cause anny othe to be geven in your name by anny person vnder the degre of a Provost except it be your vsher wch is your deputie for that tyme so longe as his covenāt doth laste wth you/ And he that you do appoynt in that rome oughte to be knowne a sufficient hable and honest parson as well by the other maisters as by your selfe for that he is a Provost licenced during his covenant with you being placed in yt rome.

16. ITEM you shall not alowe or able anny Provosts licenc wthout the consent of two maisters at the leste besydes your selfe And you shall not compact with anny person vnder couller or deceipte to kepe schole for you or in your name so that he or they shall have the proffit thearof and you beare the name by which meanes other maisters and Provosts wch stoode in place for it have their livings taken from them but you shall farther do your dilligenc and goodwill to the apprehendinge and puttinge downe of all soch as do take vppon them to teach without sufficient licences or lawful authoritie to the great sclander and hinderance of our scienc."

Students who successfully negotiated their maisters' prizing were issued with the relevant teaching certificate. This was called, naturally enough, a maisters letter. Although it was very similar in format and content to that awarded to provosts there were differences and for that reason the maisters letter is reproduced below:

"A Maisters Letter

"BE IT KNOWNE vnto all men by this present writing wheaersoever it shall come to be read hearde or vnderstanded and especially to all manner of officers vnder the dominions of our soveraigne Ladye Quene of England ffranc and Ireland defendor of the faith and in earth (next vnder Christe) of the churche of England and also of Irelande the supreame hed/ as Justices Maiors Sheriffs Bayliffs Counstables Hedboroughs and to there Deputies, certifienge you by theis our letters. That it pleaseth our saide soveraigne Ladye the Quenes ma^tie with her moste honorable counsell to admitt with authoritie and by especiall Commission vnder her highnes broade Seall to geve licence vnto all vs beinge maisters of Defence playinge with all manner of weapons vsuall And also to admitt all soch to instructe and teach from henseforth, and to admitt all maisters and Provosts to teache havinge couninge sufficient and beinge experte, and tryed before the maisters of the saide scienc openly within the Cittye of London, geving all schollers warninge xiiij dayes And then to playe his prize with so many schollers as will come that daye AND also he to challendge all Provosts gevinge them xxj dayes warning and thear to abyde the triall of so many Provosts as will playe that daye for his maisters[1] priz And then playinge his priz with so many maisters as will playe Gevinge them a monethes warning And thus doinge openly in London before all the maisters/ with all dueties that belonge to a maister Then we the saide maisters R.W: T.W: G.F. and, A.R: of the saide scienc of Defence within the Citye of London do admit E.B. maister of the said scienc the ffive and twentithe day of Maye in anno &c in so much as the saide E, did playe his priz with vs the saide maisters AND we do also admit the saide E to teache and instructe in anny place within the Queenes dominions as an hable well tryed and sufficient man with divers weapons as the longe sworde &c AND THEARFORE we the saide masters admitted by the Quenes ma^tie and her moste honorable Counsell, desyer all her highnes true subiects to ayde the said E.B: agaynst all strangers and soch as teach without authoritie, and soch forsworne men agaynst God and the Quenes ma^tie wch of longe tyme have deceaved her highnes true subiects wheaerfore we the saide RW. TW. GF. and AR. beinge four ancient maisters of this scienc w^thin the citie of London desier all her ma^ties true subiects and officers as they love god and our saide soveraigne Ladye/ to suffer none to kepe anny schole of Defenc whatsoever he be excepte he have authoritie to show in like case as this m^r EB hath In so

---

[1] This is an error in the original manuscript and should read 'Provost'.

doinge you shall shew your selves true & faithfull officers & subiects vnto your power/ thankes be geven to God for the maynteyninge of the trueth whearof we be maisters of defenc In witnes whearof &c."

These documents provide ample proof of the integrity and dedication of the maisters and their students, as well as providing an interesting insight into their beliefs and attitudes. They also leave us with no alternative but to recognise the fact that they, their schools, and their organizations were the equivalent of, and equal to, the martial arts masters and schools of Asia.

3 PRIZES AND CHALLENGES

The opening chapters contain several references to prizes and the playing of them. Prizing was English martial art's equivalent of the gradings of Asian martial arts systems. That the English martial artist referred to such an examination as a prize was typical of contemporary social attitudes. Those bold, rumbustious, and, dare one say, contentious people saw such events not merely as proof of knowledge but as contests to be fought and won, contests in which a brave performance would win them the prize of promotion and the respect of their peers.

The playing of a prize was an event which the maisters regarded as being of the utmost importance, not just for the applicant but for the organisation itself. Accordingly, prizes were played publicly, not only that people might witness for themselves the high standards set by the maisters but also to prove that the examinations were honestly conducted.

As we have seen, the basic or beginner's rank in a schole of fence was that of scholler. The manner of, and rules for, a scholler's enrolment are contained in, *The ruills and constitucons of the schole.* The number of weapons at which the scholler trained was, in most cases, two. There were, however, cases of schollers who trained at three weapons. The rules of the Company appear to give the student some choice in this matter in stating:

> …for soch weapon or weapons as the same scholler or schollers shall be willing to learn.

Unlike the higher ranks there was no minimum time span before the scholler could play his prize, it was left to his own judgement. However, the Company of Maisters, no doubt mindful of ambition's delusive powers, demanded proof of the scholler's readiness to attempt the prize. This took the form of a private test which required that he demonstrated his skill with the longsword and backsword against a minimum of six schollers in order that his proficiency might be assessed. If his efforts were successful the Four Ancient Maisters would nominate a date and venue for the playing of his prize. It then fell to the applicant to publicly announce his forthcoming test by posting Bills of Challenge, in and around the City of London. The records of the maisters themselves do not, unfortunately, contain any examples of such a document. However, it seems that the playwright Ben Jonson used such a bill as a vehicle for a comic sketch contained in his play, *Cynthia's Revels* (Act v, Sc.II). Jonson has Amorphus saying the following:

> Be it known to all that profess courtship, by these presents (from the white silk reveller, to the cloth of tissue and bodkin) that we, Ulysses-Polytropus-Amorphus master of the subtile science of courtship, do give leave and licence to our provost, Acolastus-Polypragmon-Asotus, to play his master's prize, against all masters whatsoever, in this subtile mystery, at these four, the choice and most cunning weapons of court-compliment, viz. the BARE ACCOST; the BETTER REGARD; the SOLEMN ADDRESS; and the PERFECT CLOSE. These are therefore to give notice to all comers, that he, the said Acolastus-Polypragmon-Asotus, is here present (by the help of his mercer, tailor, milliner, semster, and so forth) at his designed hour, in this fair gallery, the present day of this present month, to perform and do his uttermost for the achievement and bearing away of the prizes,...

Ben Jonson (1573–1637) might be called a realist in literary terms and is well known for presenting life as he knew it. Since schools of fence were prevalent during his lifetime we may suppose that the above cameo is, allowing for artistic licence, a reasonable representation of an actual bill of challenge. It might, therefore, prove interesting to rewrite his sketch, keeping the salient points and replacing the others with names and details which, for this purpose, are taken *ad hoc* from the Company's records:

> Be it known to all that profess skill in the science of defence that we, Richarde Beste, Roberte Polmorth, Humphrey Basset, and John Legge being the four ancient maisters of the said science of defence within the city of London, do give leave and licence to our provost, Willyam Hunt, to play his maister's prize, against all maisters whatsoever, in this subtile mystery, at these four cunning weapons of defence, viz. the long sword, the bastard sword, the backsword, and the staff. These are therefore to give notice to all comers that he, the said Willyam Hunt, is here present at his designed hour, at the Leaden Hall, the present day of the present month, to perform and do his uttermost for the achievment and bearing away of the prize.

The form of a bill of challenge, as above assumed, varies little , in essence, to one that was issued by a stage-gladiator in 1712:

> I, James Miller, serjeant, (lately come from the frontiers of Portugal), Master of the Noble Science of Defence, hearing in most Places where I have

been of the great Fame of Timothy Buck of London, Master of the said Science, do invite him to meet me, and exercise at the several weapons following, viz.

Back-Sword,	Single Falchons,
Sword and Dagger,	Case of Falchons,
Sword and Buckler,	Quarter-staff.

Stage-gladiators only had to fight the particular person they had challenged whereas the prizors of earlier days would have to fight as many people as 'Answered' their Bills of Challenge. The maisters, with customary efficiency, put the terms and conditions of the schollers prize in writing so that there could be no confusion or dispute about the procedure:

"The Order for playinge of a [Free] Schollers Prize.

"FIRST THAT EUERY Scholler at his first entrye to playe a priz shall geve his owne maister (wch he is sworne vnto) knowledge of his mynde what he doth intend to do as touchinge his priz/ And then his maister to let the other anchiant maisters vnderstand his schollers pretence concerninge his sayde priz And vppon the agrement and conclusion of the sayd maisters, the sayd scholler shalbe content in anny schole or other place whearesoever the sayd anchiant maisters shall appoyncte, to play wth vj schollers at the leste at the longe sword and backe sword for a tryall or profe, to se whether he be hable to goe forwards in his priz, or not, And so if they fyend him hable and sufficient in that behalfe/ That then as the sayd anchiant maisters shall agree and conclude to appoyncte and set his daye when he shall playe his priz, and when that daye is come/ the sayde scholler shall at the longe sworde play with so manye schollers as will playe with him that Daye And the nexte day wch shall be appoyncted, to playe at his other weapon with so manye schollers as will play that day according as the sayd anchient maisters will permit and suffer him/ AND SO to stand and agree vnto all manner of orders constitutions and agreements which the sayd ffour anchiant maisters will that he should observe and keepe And farther to pay all orders and duetyes wch belongith to soche a scholler/ MORE OVER the sayde scholler after he hathe playd his schollers priz and is admitted a free scholler by the maisters/ shall not at anny tyme within the space of seven years after his sayd admittance attempte or endevor to speake vnto anny maister or maisters concerninge anny other priz vntill the sayde seven yeares shall be fully expyred And then if he be mynded to play his Provost priz/to do as hearafter followeth

VIUAT REGINA."

Some confusion exists as to how many bouts the prizor was expected to perform against each of his challengers, the matter having previously been the subject of some debate. One belief is that he was expected to fight three bouts with each weapon against each 'Answerer'. The alternative hypothesis is that the number of bouts required was two. It is a subject about which the official rules of the Company say nothing, presumably because the number of bouts fought was so well known at the time that it was felt unnecessary to specify the information. It is not possible, with any confidence, to plump for one or the other. Jonson, whose words were used to recreate the bill of challenge, provides clear support for the two bout hypothesis when he has Hedon announce (*Cynthia's Revels*, Act V, Scene III)

"This weapon is done."

To which Amorphus replies:

"No, we have two bouts at every weapon."

Again, a little later, Amorphus says:

"The second bout, to conclude the weapon."

If we accept Jonson's description of a bill of challenge it would seem churlish not to accept his information relating to the number of bouts fought. He was, after all, a contemporary of the maisters of defence. Nevertheless, an entry in the Company's files would appear to contradict him. This occurs in the record of Gregorie Grene's provost prize, which mentions one of his opponents, Izake Kennard, only playing two bouts with the long sword because of an injured hand. The very fact that this detail was recorded suggests that two bouts was not the norm. Robert Triphooks's *Miscellanie Antiqua Anglicana*, published 1816, contains a fascinating tale from the reign of Henry VIII concerning the marvellous Long Meg of Westminster that seems to support the three bout theory. Long Meg was furious at a man named Woolner who had eaten her other guests' breakfasts and refused to pay for more than one. In her anger Long Meg challenged Woolner to:

take that staffe and have a bout with me for thy breakfast, hee that gives the first three Venies scape free;...

Further support for this hypothesis comes from the pen of George Silver, a contemporary, though probably amateur, maister of defence who, in suggesting a way to test a foreign master's proficiency to teach arms in England, says that they should fight three bouts apiece with three of the best English maisters of defence. Unfortunately the problem is not that easily solved since, in another part of his work, Silver tells us, when condemning the principles and methods of Vincentio Saviolo (see p.58), that:

> And againe, for proofe that there is no truth, neither in his rules, grounds or Rapier-fight, let triall be made in this maner: Set two vnskilfull men together at the Rapier and Dagger, being valiant, and you shall see, that once in two bouts there shall either one or both of them be hurt. Then set two skilfull men together, being valiant at the Rapier and Dagger, and they shall do the like…

Given the critical context in which Silver was writing it is entirely possible that he deliberately chose two bouts to highlight his argument. That is to say that the methods and principles of which he wrote were so bad that anyone using them had a one in two chance of being hurt, or, to put it another way, only had a fifty-fifty chance of winning. At any rate, later writers, such as Samuel Pepys, testify that stage-gladiators, in his time at least, fought three bouts with each weapon.

However, from the eighteenth century onwards, it appears from contemporary accounts that it was quite common for stage-gladiators to fight two bouts apiece with each weapon as opposed to three. This is born out by reports that the audiences, whether by right or custom, would call for the fighters to change to a different weapon after two bouts. It is not an easy problem to solve, apart from the conflicting evidence there are also many imponderable factors; did the custom change over a period of time? Did the number of bouts fought depend on the rank being striven for? Was three the maximum and two the minimum, with judges having the right to call a halt after two satisfactorily performed bouts (traditionally known as 'best of three')? The above mentioned problems and possibilities notwithstanding, it seems that, as far as the traditional maisters of defence were concerned, the evidence errs somewhat in favour of three bouts.

The total number of bouts fought by prizors depended not only on the two or three bout supposition but also, of course, on how many people accepted the challenge. The records show that one prizor had 42 separate fights, at three bouts per weapon that represents a total of 126 bouts, or, at two bouts per weapon, 84 bouts. Though the bouts were spread over two days it was still an incredible feat of strength, courage, and skill. The enormity of the prizor's task is all the more impressive when it is remembered that he was, in effect, fighting non-stop, whereas his opponents were always fresh and rested. It must be remembered also that the manner of winning a bout was to land a blow on your opponent. It follows that you lost a bout by receiving a blow. Bruising, bleeding, and the occasional broken bone were the painful result of being hit by the heavy weapons of the day. In terms of sheer physical effort the free schollers prize was probably the hardest, since at that level there were usually plenty of answerers. The higher the rank the fewer the students to answer the challenge.

The following examples from the official records of the Company of Maisters provide graphic evidence of the immense effort required of the prizor.

"EDWARD HARVYE playde his schollers priz at the Bull within Bishopps gate at ij weapons, the two hande sworde and the sword and buckeler Thear playde with him xiiij at the two hand sworde and xxviij at sworde and buckeler/ with two free schollers called Rayson, and ffrauncies Caverly/ the xxviij of January vnder Richard Smyth.

"WILLIAM MATHEW playde his schollers priz at the Bull within Bishopps gate at two kynd of weapons the two hand sword and the backe sworde. Theare playd wth him xij at the two hand sword and xvj at the backe sworde/ and one fre scholler whose name was ffrancies Calverly/ The vj of maye and so was admitted free scholler vnder Willyam Thompson als Glover.

"JOHN BLINKENSOPPS playde his schollers priz vnder Willyam Glover at Burntwode in Essex at iij weapons the longe sworde, the backe sworde, and sword and buckeler and thear playde with him x at longe sworde xij at backe sworde and xviij at sworde and buckeler But he was not admitted, by cause of misdemenor by him committed and for want of his games wch weare not in place/ He was allowed a fre scholler the Tenth of Juyn at the Kings hed at Pye corner by Wm Joyner Ric: Donne Ric: Smythe and W: Mucklow.

"THOMAS NOBLE playde his schollers prize at the Bull within Bishoppsgate the sixth day of ffebruary at two weapons That is to say the longe sword and the sworde and buckeler thear playd with him at longe sworde x/ and two fre schollers/ at the sword and buckeler xxij bysids the ij fre schollers whose names weare Willyam Mathew wch playd at both weapons and John Grene who playd at longe sword & no more And so the sayde Thomas Noble was admittet vnder Gregory Greene mr/1578.

"ROBERT BLISSE playd his schollers priz at the Bull in Bishopps gate the fiveth day of Juyn at two kynde of weapons That is to say the two hand sworde and the sworde and buckeler Thear playde with him three at the two hand sworde and 16 at the sworde and buckeler And three fre schollers at both weapons That is to saye John Harris Valentyn Longe and John Dawell and so the said Robert Blisse was admitted a fre scholler vnder Richard Smyth m^r 1581/.

"ROGER HORNE playde his schollers priz at Oxforde at two kinde of weapons that is to saye the two hand sword and the sword and buckeler Thear playde with him five at the two hand sword and viij at the sworde and buckeler with iiij free schollers That is to say John Blinkinsopps ffrauncies Caverly Edward Harvie and Willyam Mathewe/ the 25 day of May and so was admitted vnder Willyam Mucklow maister.

Those schollers who succeeded in 'bearing away' the prize were granted the rank of free scholler. According to the rules they had to remain at this rank for seven years (though there were exceptions to this) before they could apply to play their provost's prize. As was the case with the scholler's prize, the rules for this were laid down by the maisters:

"The Order of a Provost's Prize.

"IMPRIMIS THAT every free scholler which is mynded to proceede to anny other degree of the noble scyenc of Defence, to be a provoste, shall first desyer his owne maisters goodwill/ And then his maister and he together shall goe to the four anchiant maisters and informe them of his Provosts priz and that he is willing to play it AND yf it chance that the free schollers maister whom he was sworne vnto be dceased, that then the sayde free scholler shall chose for his m^r one of the ancient maisters to play his Provosts priz vnder which he hath moste mynd vnto And shall be sworne to him as he was to his first maister in all poyncts/ And accordinge as the four ancient maisters shall agree together and conclude of the matter so he to goe forward with his provosts priz, so that he be contented to abyde all manner of orders wch the ancient maysters will that he shold kepe, and to make them an obligacon of the same and to sett to his hand and Seall as the maysters will that he shold do in all poyncts/ IN SO DOINGE the four ancyent maisters to appoyncte his day, and when he shall playe his Provosts priz/ And he to play at the two hand sword, the backe sword, and staffe with all manner of Provosts which do come into that place to play with him And allso the sayd free scholler shall at his owne proper Costs go and geve warning to all the Provosts which ar within three score myles of the place wheare he is appoynctd to play his Provosts prize That they may come to his priz wheare he doth play it, and so to play with him, and every Provost wch is within thre score myles that hath no warning to come to

45

his prizes the sayd free scholler shall pay to the ancient maisters fyve shillings of lawfull mony of England And yf theire be no Provost to play with him And for to geve them iiij weickes warning at the leaste before the Day become which the maisters have sett him And as many Provosts as do dwell farther then Twentye myles That then the free scholler shall paye the one halfe of thear Charges Thus doinge when the appoyncted day is come to proceede in his sayd priz And to make his Provosts Lc̄e, payinge to the four ancient maisters for sealling thearof after the rate wch is set amongst them with all manner of other Duetyes belonginge to them AND more over he to be bowned to the iiij ancient maisters not to keepe anny scholle within the space of seven myles of anny maister, without speciall leave of the sayd four ancient maisters And allso to be bound in his sayd obligacon not to teach anny scholler this noble scyenc of defenc xcepte he doth sweare him vnto his owne maister whom he was sworne himselfe And farther he be bownd to pay vnto his sayd maister (to whom he is sworne) for every scholler wch he shall teache, to pay xijd And so in lik wyes to the most ancient mayster of the four sayd And to yeald vp his true accoumpt onc in every quarter of a yeare AND ALLSO yf he Dwell with in the space of thre skore myles wheare anny Provosts priz is or shall be playde havinge warning or knowledge thearof Then to come and play at the same priz without anny Lett vppon payne of payinge vj^s viij^d vnto the fower ancient maisters/ except he be sicke in bodye or other wyes busied in the Queens affayers AND FINALLYE he to be bound in his obligac̄on aforesayd vnto the four ancient maisters,

The following examples of provosts prizes have been taken from the official records of the maisters:

"John Evanes als Gerkinmaker playd his provosts prize in Hartford vnder Willyam Glover als Thompson at thre weapons the longe sword, the backe sword and the sword and buckeler/ with two provosts, Willyam Mucklowe and Richard Smythe/ He playd his schollers prize att Baldocke in Hartfordshire at two weapons/ vidz with seven at the longe sword, and six at sword and buckeler.

"Izake Kennard playd his provosts priz at the Bull within Bishopps gate the vij^th of June at thre weapons, the longe sword, the sword and buckeler, and the staff/ Ther playd wth him two free schollers for want of Provosts/ Willyam Wilks/ and ffrancis Calverte/ vnder Richard Smyth in anno dni/1575/

"Gregorie Grene playd his provosts priz the five-tenth daye of October at the Bull within Bishopps gate at thre weapons the longe sword, the backe sword, and the sword and buckeler Ther playde with him two provosts/ Izake Kennard and Willyam Wilks, Izake had a sore hand and so he playd but twice at longe sword/ And so the sayd Gregorie was made provoste vnder Willyam Mucklowe.

"John Blinkinsopps playd his provosts priz the nyneth daye of June at the Bull within Bishoppsgate at thre weapons the longe sword, the backe sword, and the staff There playd with him John Goodwyne a provost and ffrancis Calverte a fre scholler, which had a provosts licence for that tyme And so John Blinkinsopps was made provoste vnder Willyam Thompson als Glover.

"Edward Harvie playd his provosts priz the five and twentith daye of August at the Theatour at thre weapons the two hand sword the backe sword and the sword and buckeler There playd with him one Provoste whose name is John Blinkinsopp/And one fre scholler called by name ffrancis Calvert who had a Provosts lysence for that tyme And so the sayd Edward Harvye was made a provoste vnder Richard Smythe maister/1578/

"Thomas Pratt did agre with the maisters And was made Provost the seventh daye of Juyne vnder Gregorye Greene/ maister/ 1582/

"Roberte Blisse playde his Provosts prize at the Theator in Holiwell the first day of Julye at thre weapons/ the longe sword the backe sworde and the sword and buckeler Their playde with him thre Provosts vidz Alexander Reyson, Thomas Prat and Valentine Longe And so the sayd Robert Blisse was admitted Provoste vnder Richard Smyth/ 1582/

"Vallentine Longe playde his provosts priz at the Courten in Holiwell the fiveth daye of August at thre weapons the longe sworde, the backe sword and the sworde and buckeler Theire playd with him two Provosts vidz Roberte Blisse and Androwe Bello: And John Dewell who had a Provosts licence for that tyme And so the sayd Valentyne Longe was admitted provost vnder Gregorye Grene/ m^r/ 1582/

"John Dewell playd h[is] challenge at the theator in Holiwell agaynste all Provosts and free schollers at thre weapons, the longe sword the sword and buckeler and the sword and dagger Their playd with him Thomas Pratt, Roberte Blisse & Androw Bello, Provosts Valentyne Longe John Harris, Willyam Otte, and George Muckelowe free schollers And the sayde John Dewell was not admitted Provoste at that tyme for his disorder But he was alowed provoste by the goodwills of the maysters the Tenth day of Auguste vnder Willyam Joyner/ 1582/

The final prize to be played was for the rank of maister, the rules for which are given below:

"The Order for Playinge of a Maisters Prize,

"WHEN ANNY PROVOST is mynded to take the degree of a m^r That is, to play a maisters priz he shall first declare his mynd vnto his m^r, vnder whom he playd his Provosts priz, yf he be livinge/ and yf he be ded then shall he chuse for his maister one of the four ancient maisters, to play his priz vnder, whom he liketh best And shall be sworne vnto him, as he was to his first maister And then shall he desyer his maisters favor for the playinge of his sayd maisters priz and so to crave the good Wills of all the ancient maisters of the noble scienc of Defenc And accordinge as the ancient maisters do agree in that cause, he to procede in his sayd priz SO THAT he will be content to agree vnto them, and to all their orders and ruills accordinge as they have amongste them And never survince or invent by anny kynd of meanes to put anny maister of that noble scienc to anny displeasure or hinderanc, but shall be contented to fulfill all their constitucōns orders and ruills to the vttermost of his power, And shall byend himselfe in an obligacōn to the iiij ancient m^{rs} for performanc therof AND so doinge the sayd maisters shall appoynct him his day, wheare he shall play his maisters priz/ at theis weapons followinge vidz the two hand sword, the Basterd sword, the pike, the backe sword, and the rapier and Dagger And then the sayd provost, to gev warninge to so many maisters as dwell within xl myles of the place appoyncted for his priz, eight weikes at the lest, before the day cometh to play his priz AND WHEN he hath playd his maisters priz he then to mak his maisters Lēē and pay for the sealling of it to thancient maisters, wth all manner duetys to them belonging And so to byend him selfe in an obligacōn to the sayd ancient maisters to fulfill all that is abovesayd and to set his hand and seall thearvnto, Those done the four ancient maisters to gev him his maisters othe with all things that apperteyneth to the same."

The following examples of maisters' prizings are of extra importance because they bear witness to the interest shown by English monarchs in the affairs of the maisters of defence.

"Richarde White played his maisters priz at the graye ffriers wthin Nuegate at thre kinde of weapons, that is to say, the longe sworde, the Basterde sword and the Backsworde with thre maisters, vidz Willyam Hunte, Peter Beste, and Willyam Browne, And he plaid his Provosts priz at Leaden Hall with two Provosts, that is to saye Edward Brytten and John Barsett at thre kinde of weapons vidz the longe sworde, the backesword and the staffe. He plaide his Schollers priz at Leaden Hall with xxiij schollers at the backesword and at Hampton Courte wth xiiij at the longe sworde.

"Thomas Weaver was made maister by Kinge Edward the sixthe at Grenwitche.

"Roberte Edmonds played his maisters priz at the Whitehall before kinge Phillipp and Quene Marie at thre kind of weapons that is to saye, the longe sworde, the backesworde and the staffe thear played agaynste him two maisters vidz Richard White and Thomas Weaver.

"Izake Kennard came into the place to play his maisters priz at the Bull w^thin Bishopps gate the one and twentith daye of Apprill at four kynde of weapons That is to saye the two hand sword the backe sworde the sword and buckeler and the rapier and dagger/ ther playde with him thre maisters vidz Gregorie Grene Willyam Mucklowe and Willyam Joyner/ The sayd Izake playde with the thre maisters at the longe sworde/ and was stroken downe at the backe sworde by Willyam Muckelowe and so was dismiste for that tyme/ The said Izake came the Mondaye after and playd the reste of his weapons, that is to saye the sword and buckeler and the rapier and dagger/. ther playde with him the thre maisters aforesayd vidz Gregorye Grene, William Muckelowe and Willyam Joyner the 28 daye of Aprill and so the sayde Izake was by entreatye made mayster vnder Richarde Smyth mayster the Tenthe daye of Maye/1578.

"John Blinkinsop playd his maisters prize the firste daye of June at the Artillerye garden at four kynde of weapons That is to saye the two hand sword, the backe sword, the sword and buckeler and the staff Ther playd with him six maisters vidz Richard Peters/ Anthonye ffenruther/ Gregorie Grene, Richard Smyth Richard Donne & Henrye Naylor And so the said Blinkinsop was admitted maister vnder Willyam Thompson maister/1579/.

"Willyam Mathewes playd his maisters prize at Canterburye ye fiveth day of June at four kynde of weapons That is to saye the longe sworde the back sworde the sworde and buckeler and the rapier and dagger, ther playd wth him 8 maisters vidz ffranceis Calverte, John Blinkinsop, John Goodwin, Izake Kennard, Gregorye Grene, John Evans, Richard Smith, and Henrye Naylor And so was admitted m^r vnder Richard Peter/1583/

English martial artists of this period, like some of their modern counterparts, loved the thrill of competitions which they called challenges. The records of the maisters contain notes of these events:

"FIRSTE a challenge playde at Hampton Courte by Willm̄ Pascall, Richarde White, and Robert Edmonde before king Henry the eighte at three sundrey kynde of weapons, that is to saye the longe sworde, the backe sworde, and the staffe agaynst all Provoste and Maisters wch challenge was alowed, a schollers prize for the saide Richarde White.

"ITEM a challenge playde at Grenwich before king Edwarde the sixthe by Willyam Pascall and vj schollers challengers the same Willm̄ agaynste all maisters and the other six agaynste all schollers commers at six kynde of weapons vidz the maisters at the axe, the Pike, the longe sworde, the backe sworde, the basterde sword and the rapier and dagger The vj schollers at thre kynde of weapons, the longe sworde, the backe sworde and the staffe.

"ITEM a challenge playde before the kings ma^tie at westminster by three maisters willyam Pascall Robert Grene and Willm̄ Browne at seven kynde of weapons That is to say the axe, the pyke, the rapier, the dagger, the rapier and target the rapier and cloke and ii[hand] sworde agaynst all alyens and strangers beinge borne without the kings Dominions of what countrie Soever he or they weare gevinge them warninge by their bille set up by the three maisters the space of eighte weeks before the sayd challenge was playde and it was holden four severall sundayes one after another/

"ITEM a challenge playde at westminster before King Philip and Quene Marie by Richarde White maister, at tenne kynde of weapons Thear playde with him fower That is to say Willyam Hunt Thomas Weaver Roberte Edmonde and Willyam Hearne

"ITEM a challenge playde at westminster before Quene Elizabeth by Richarde White, Willyam Hearne and Roberte Edmonde challengers and theare playde Thomas Weaver againste Richarde White and Willm̄ Hearne/ and Willyam Joyner agaynste Roberte Edmonde.

There are other entries of challenges (and prizes) in the records of the maisters but at this point it may prove interesting to step forward in time and examine a few challenges recorded in the days of the stage-gladiators. These later descriptions of challenges tend to give more details of the fighters and their methods. The 1775 compilation of Grose's *Antiquarian Repertory* contains a translation of notes, published in 1672, by Jorevin de Rochefort that describes a fight between stage-gladiators that he had witnessed during a visit to England:

> We went to see the Bergiardin [Beargarden], which is a great amphitheatre where combats are fought between all sorts of animals, and sometimes men (as we once saw). Commonly when any fencing-masters are desirous of showing their courage and their great skill, they issue mutual challenges, and before they engage, parade the town with drums and trumpets sounding, to inform the public that there is a challenge between two brave masters of the science of defence, and that the battle will be fought on such a day. We went to see this combat, which was performed on a stage in the middle of this amphitheatre, where, on the flourishes of trumpets and the beat of drums, the combatants entered, stripped to their shirts. On a signal from the drum, they drew their swords, and immediately began the fight, skirmishing a long time without any wounds; they were both very skilful and courageous: the tallest had the advantage over the least; for according to the English fashion of fencing, they endeavoured rather to cut than push in the French manner, so that by his height he had the advantage of being able to strike his antagonist on the head, against which the little one was on his guard; he had in his turn an advantage over the great one, in being able to give him the Jarnac stroke, by cutting him on his right ham, which he left in a manner quite unguarded, so that, all things considered, they were equally matched; nevertheless, the tall one struck his antagonist on the wrist, which he almost cut off; but this did not prevent him from continuing the fight, after he had been dressed, and taken a glass or two of wine to give him courage, when he took ample vengeance for his wound; for a little afterwards making a feint at the ham, the tall man stooping, in order to parry it, laid his whole head open, when the little one gave him a stroke which took off a slice of his head, and almost all his ear... The surgeons immediately dressed them, and bound up their wounds, which being done they resumed their combat, and both being sensible of their respective disadvantages, they therefore were a long time without giving or receiving a wound, which was the cause that the little one, failing to parry so exactly, being tired with this long battle, received a stroke on his wounded wrist, which dividing the sinews, he remained vanquished, and the tall conqueror received the applause of all the spectators.

Another account of a challenge between stage-gladiators comes to us from the pen of Herr von Uffenbach who was in England in 1710:

In the afternoon we drove to the Bear-Garden at Hockley-in-the-Hole to watch the fights that take place there, a truly English amusement. First a properly printed challenge was carried round and dealt out. Not only were all the conditions of the fight there set forth, but also the weapons to be used. The combatants were an Englishman and a Moor. . . The former was called Thomas Wood and the latter George Turner. The Moor is by profession a fencing master; . . . The place where the fight took place was fairly large. In the middle was a platform as tall as a man of middling height; it had no rail and was open all round, so that neither of the fighters could retreat...

Then the master and the fighter I mentioned above appeared themselves. They had taken off their coats and tied only a handkerchief round their heads. First they bowed in every direction, and then showed their swords all round. These were very broad and long and uncommonly sharp. Each of the combatants had his second by him with a large stick in his hand; they were not there to parry blows, but only to see that there was fair play on all sides. They began the fight with broadswords. The Moor got the first wound, above the breast, which bled not a little. Then the onlookers began to cheer and call for Wood; they threw down vast quantities of shillings and crowns, which were picked up by his second... In the second round the Englishman, Wood, took a blow above the loins of such force that, not only did his shirt hang in tatters, but his sword was knocked out of his hand, and all the buttons on one side of the open breeches he wore were cut away.

Then they went for each other with sword and dagger, and the Moor got a nasty wound in the hand, which bled freely. It was probably due to this that, when they attacked each other twice with 'sword-and-buckler', that is to say with broadsword and shield, the good Moor received such a dreadful blow that he could not fight any longer. He was slashed from the left eye right down his cheek to his chin and jaw with such force that one could hear the sword grating against his teeth. Straightway not only the whole of his shirt front but the platform too was covered with blood. The wound gaped open as wide as a thumb, and I cannot tell you how ghastly it looked on the black face. A barber-surgeon immediately sprang towards him and sewed up the wound, while the moor stood there without flinching. When this had been done and a cloth bound round his head, the Moor would have liked to continue with the fight, but, since he had bled so profusely, neither the surgeon nor the seconds, who act as umpires, would allow this. So the combatants shook hands (as the did after each round) and prepared to get down.

There are many such descriptions of challenges in the days of the stage-gladiators but to include any more might seem to be praising the gore that went with their glory. However, the examples given prove that commercial martial arts were almost as dangerous as the battle-field version from which they sprang.

4   THE BROADSWORD

In man's long and destructive history he has invented many weapons that are superior to the sword as an instrument of death. Yet few of them command as much esteem in our folk-lore as does the sword. Tales of magic, romance, and derring-do cut a swathe through our imagination as keenly as the sword itself sliced through human flesh. From Iceland to China, from the knights of Camelot to the heroes of Hollywood, the level of veneration achieved by the sword aptly reflects the powerful emotions that have polished the reputation of this weapon of weapons.

Yet it is still not easy to reconcile our reverence for this weapon with its actual battlefield value. That it was an effective fighting weapon cannot be denied. However, that is not to say that it was the best or the most favoured of weapons. For example, in Germanic society when males attained the necessary age and fighting proficiency they were presented with a spear and shield. The comparative cheapness of the spear compared to the sword was an important factor but it was quite common for swordsmen also to be armed with spears, only drawing their swords if the spear was broken, or if the enemy got to close quarters. Saxo appears to give some support to this view when he relates in *Starkad's Vow* that:

> Three armed with clubs came first, and three armed with swords behind,
> and three with spears were last.

His words seem to suggest an ascending order of importance, with the clubmen, as the least effective, attacking first, and the spearmen, as the most dangerous, attacking last. The supposition applied to Saxo's words appear to be justified by advice contained in the *Speculum Regale*, a treatise containing information about the military methods and armaments of the northern European peoples. This work, purportedly written in the twelfth century, contained the following advice:

> ...take care lest you entangle your shield; take care likewise lest your spear
> is snatched from you, unless you have two, for in an engagement on foot,
> one spear is better than two swords.

As well as the spear, the battleaxe and bill often took battlefield precedence over the sword. Nevertheless, the fact remains that none of those weapons has ever attained the status with which history has sheathed the sword.

It seems, therefore, that we must look for additional reasons for the sword's importance. This approach finds us considering, for example, the actual manufacture of the weapon. It would be no exaggeration to say that for many generations the swordsmith's art was looked upon as a mystery akin to, indeed associated with, the magical arts. In other words it was a process which few knew or understood. Given this circumstance it should come as no surprise that people genuinely believed that swords were made by magicians such as the dwarves of Svartalfheim or Wayland the Smith.[1]

Given that our superstitious ancestors believed in sorcery it is not too difficult to understand their belief that the sword itself could be enchanted, to contain, as it were, a spirit of its own. A spirit that could aid or hinder the wielder of the weapon as it saw fit. It could misdirect the cutting edge of his blade or alternatively render him invincible. It was even believed that the 'spirit' of the sword could transfer the courage and wisdom of one owner to another. The origin and powers of Excalibur, as related in the tales of King Arthur (themselves based on much older heathen traditions), are good examples of this 'magical' belief.

Of course in seeking a reason for mans' 'worship' of the sword we mustn't overlook his pecuniary motives. It cannot be denied that humankind has ever worshipped that which is valuable. Swords could be enormously expensive and for that reason were usually associated with the rich and powerful. The only way that others were likely to come by a sword was to pluck it from a fallen opponent or to be given one as a gift. Such a costly weapon was not given lightly and to qualify for such an honour a man had to be of considerable importance to his leader. For example, he may have performed some pleasing feat, or shown himself to be a mighty warrior. Ultimately the giving of a sword by a king or chieftain came to symbolise a mutual bond of loyalty and friendship, even unto death itself.

It is clear that, quite apart from its military value, the sword became an emblem of wealth, power and mysticism, and this explains why it was utilised in so many social and ceremonial roles. It is held for example to represent mercy in kingship and justice in law, as well as being used to confer knighthood. In times past the sword was also linked with oath-taking of various kinds. For example, when a man swore loyalty to his king, or, during wedding ceremonies when couples would mutually swear fidelity upon the hilt of the sword. Such oaths suggest that the sword had obtained Christian symbolism to go along with the secular. A ceremony which was practised in England at least as early as the sixteenth century gives a clue as to the origin of this added authority. The ceremony was that of swearing the provost's oath, the relevant part of which follows:

---

[1] Characters from Germanic mythology.

...and by the Crosse of this sworde whiche dothe represent vnto you the crosse wch our saviour Jesus Christe did suffer his moste paynefull deathe and passion vppon for our redemption.

The sword we are dealing with is the broadsword, a weapon that reigned supreme for so long in Europe and even longer in England. Indeed so strong was the Englishman's love for this weapon that it was also known as the Saxon Blade. The English insisted on using it long after it had fallen out of favour on the continent where it was largely replaced by the rapier and its derivatives. The instinct of the English warrior was sound because experience proved that the rapier was only of use when pitched against another rapier. This is borne out by the words of Turner who says:

In the time of the late Troubles[2] in England long Rapiers were used for a while and then laid aside.

The inference and the experience are clear, the rapier was rather ineffective as a weapon of war.

The rapier arrived in England as part and parcel of the Italian-inspired renaissance of the sixteenth century when it was rapidly taken up by the English gentleman as part of his social training. With the rapier arrived Italian fencing masters to teach its usage. These Italian masters took to ridiculing English fighting methods in order to promote their own. One Italian is known to have been of the opinion that English sword fighting was, 'clownish and dastardly'. Despite their high opinions of themselves the Italian masters showed a marked reluctance to accept the challenges of their English counterparts, one who did was soundly thrashed. Another boastful Italian, who repeatedly refused to fight one of the English maisters of defence of whom he was so scornful, suffered the humiliation of being punched to the ground and having a jug of beer poured over his head by his furious challenger. Another renowned Italian fencing master (Jeronimo) learned to his fatal cost the merits of the broadsword when he tangled with a certain Mister Cheese, as can be seen from the following:

He [Jeronimo] being in a coch [coach] with a wench he loved well, there was one Cheese, a verie tall man, in his fight naturall English, for he fought with his Sword and Dagger, and in Rapier-fight he had no skill at all. This Cheese having a quarrell to Jeronimo, overtooke him upon the way, himselfe being on horsebacke did call to Jeronimo and bad [bade] him come forth of the Coch or he would fetch him for he was come to fight

---

2 The English Civil War

with him. Jeronimo presently went forth of the Coch and drew his Rapier and dagger, put himself into his best ward [stance] or Stoccata, which ward was taught by himselfe and Vincentio, [Vincentio Saviolo, Jeronimo's fellow instructor] and by them best allowed of to be the best ward to stand upon in fight for life either to assault the enemie, or stand and watch his coming. Which ward it should seeme he ventured his life upon, but howsoever with all the fine Italienated skill Jeronimo had, Cheese with his Sword within two thrustes ran him into the body and slue him.

In the light of both civil and military experiences, such as those quoted above, it is hardly surprising that the English chose to remain faithful to the weapon of their forefathers. The pragmatic side of their nature would never allow them to discard a weapon that had served them so well unless an alternative could be shown to be superior. One fencing master put it quite succinctly when he said: 'The Small-Sword[3] is the Call of Honour, the Back-Sword[4] the Call of Duty.' That is to say that the former is for duelling, the latter for military conflict. Eventually the rapier/smallsword masters were to concede defeat and include the broadsword in their curriculum. Unfortunately few of them were familiar with the weapon and the methods they taught were often based on rapier or smallsword techniques: a disastrous marriage of convenience since the principles of the two weapons cannot happily share the same bed.

The techniques of broadsword fighting were, over a period of several centuries, to expand considerably. This was because the broadsword itself was the subject of considerable evolution. For the purpose of this book the main development in which we are interested is that from the blade with almost parallel edges (that is to say with a negligible taper on the blade), Figure 1, to the blade with quite sharply tapering edges, Figure 2.[5] (see opposite)

From a fighting standpoint this development brought about a radical change, perhaps we should say created radical additions, to the art of the broadsword. The weight of the sword with 'parallel' edges would, in use, focus towards the tip, whereas the weight of the tapered blade would focus nearer to the hilt. By this simple expedient the sword's centre of gravity was moved very much closer to the user's hand which allowed for greater speed and dexterity. The practical outcome of this development was that the more acutely tapered blade could be controlled by wrist actions, which in turn resulted in smaller and quicker blade

---

[3] A derivative of the rapier.

[4] A broadsword with only one cutting edge.

[5] The evolution of the sword was by no means as simple or straightforward as it might seem from the above text. Those readers interested in this subject are recommended to read specialist books such as, *The Sword in Anglo-Saxon England* by H. R. E. Davidson.

movements. The former type, generally required larger movements of the arm to wield the sword. For this reason swords of the earlier type were almost always used in conjunction with a shield. Opponents would, in effect, take turns to deliver blows. After delivering an attack the fighter would defend himself with his shield until he had a chance to aim a further blow of his own. The development of the tapered (and comparatively lighter) blade led, eventually, to a fencing system in which the sword was used for defence as well as attack. In effect the sword assumed the defensive duties of the shield by blocking with the blade either prior to or immediately following an attack. There was considerable overlap in this development. In fact the methods of the earlier broadswords were never discarded because they could still be effectively used with the later, more acutely tapered swords.

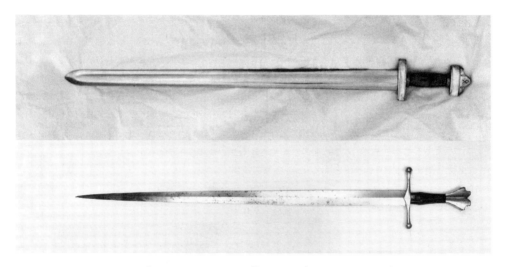

Figure 1. Top – replica Anglo-Saxon sword
overall length 39in (1mtr)– blade width 2in (5cm) – weight 2·2lb

Figure 2. Bottom – 15th century broadsword
overall length 34¾in (88·3cm) – blade width 1¾in (4·1cm) – weight 2·15lb
Photo: with thanks to the Trustees of The Wallace Collection, London

Because of the above mentioned overlap it was a long time before the shield disappeared from the scene. It was still to be found in use centuries later in conjunction with the 'new' swords though it was sometimes substituted by a dagger. That is to say that the dagger assumed, as far as was possible, the defensive duties of the shield.

Regardless of the type of blade, the broadsword, in the hands of an expert, was capable of inflicting terrible injuries. Let us take a look at a few examples of this weapon's use; examples which will illustrate both its awesome power and the incredible skill of bygone warriors.

The famous Anglo-Saxon poem Beowulf gives us a descriptive, if gory, account of a sword fight between King Ongentheow and the brothers Wulf and Eofor:

> There Ongetheow, hair streaked with grey, was brought to bay by the edges of swords, so that he, a king, might be made to submit to Eofor's sole judgement. Wulf, son of Wonred, struck Ongetheow angrily with his weapon so that streams of blood sprang forth from his head. But the aged king was not afraid and he repaid his attacker with a deadlier blow. The brave son of Wonred could not reply for Ongetheow sheared his helmet so that, blood-stained, Wulf bowed down and fell to the ground... Then Wulf's brother Eofor with his broad blade, an ancient sword of the giants, struck over the top of the shield-wall and burst the helmet which giants made. The king, protector of his people, fell, hit with a fatal blow.

It may seem unfair that two men should attack one but it was not seen that way by the combatants of those days. As long as they actually attacked one at a time it was held to be acceptable.

Fierce as the above encounter was it doesn't even begin to illustrate to the reader the gruesome efficiency that was the hallmark of the broadsword. It was not unknown for the broadsword to cut a man's body in two with one stroke. Such was the case when Prince Offa fought against two men in a duel, which took place on an island in the river Eider, when he slew both his opponents by slicing their bodies completely in half. Both the Prince and his sword Skrep were obviously formidable opponents. The Greek chronicler, Ammanius Marcellinus[6] leaves us in no doubt as to the terrible efficiency of these swords when describing injuries inflicted by them on the Romans during a battle with the Goths.

> Some again had their heads cloven in half with blows of swords, so that one side of their heads hung down on each shoulder in a most horrible manner.

Some of the best descriptions of swordplay come to us from the Icelandic Sagas. For example the Eyrbyggja Saga gives us a graphic description of a fiercely fought battle between Steinthorr and his companions, and the sons of Thorbrand, who were trapped on a rock situated in a frozen river:

> ...They were a long time attacking the reef. And when they had been fighting for a long while, Thord Bligh took a run at the reef and tried to

---

[6] Though a Roman citizen Ammanius Marcellanius was born of Greek parents.

thrust his spear into Thorleif Cimbe, for he was ever the foremost of his company. The thrust fell on Thorleif's shield, but because Thord had put all of his strength into it, his foot gave on the slippery ice-flake, and he fell on his back and slid sprawling down off the reef. Thorleif Cimbe leapt after him to try to kill him before he could get to his feet. Freystein Bove also sprang after Thorleif: he had on his spiked shoes. Steinthorr ran up and cast his shield over Thord as Thorleif was cutting at him, and with the other hand he hewed at Thorleif Cimbe and cut off his leg below the knee; but as this came to pass, Freystein Bove thrust at Steinthorr, aiming at his belly; but when Steinthorr saw that he sprang up into the air and the thrust passed between his legs, and these three feats which have now been told he did all at the same time…

Steinthorr's skills, incredible though they were, would not appear to be at all unusual. The Droplaugarson Saga, for example, records that the hero of the tale threw his sword and shield in the air and caught them in opposite hands in order to deliver a blow from a different angle. Such skills should not in any way surprise us because European martial artists are known to have honed their fighting skills as reverently as any of their Oriental counterparts. There are many historical verifications of this martial attitude but an interesting one to turn to is that given by Saxo Grammaticus, who tells us that Gram:

> …practised with the most zealous training whatsoever serves to sharpen and strengthen the bodily powers. Taught by the fencers, he trained himself by sedulous practise in parrying and dealing blows.

Saxo further relates that, by royal decree, the king's soldiers had to learn the same skills from fencing champions:

> …To save the minds of his soldiers from being melted into sloth by this inaction, he decreed that they should assiduously learn from the champions the way of parrying and dealing blows. Some of these were skilled in a remarkable manner of fighting, and used to smite the eyebrow on the enemy's forehead with an infallible stroke: but if any man, on receiving the blow, blinked for fear, twitching his eyebrow, he was at once expelled the court and dismissed the service.

A rather unique brand of skill and courage is referred to by Grose in his Antiquarian Repertory (1792). For he mentions a maister of defence by the name of Langford whom he talks of thus:

> …who being blind was yet able to teach others the Noble Science of Defence, only he desired to know the length of the weapon of his fellow

combatant with a guess at his posture, and then he practised with good success.

[Aylward, English Master of Arms...]

It was certainly an extraordinary achievement on the part of maister Langford to overcome his immense handicap. Yet we should hardly be surprised for history ever seems to suggest that the martial artist of old was a person of infinite ability and irresistible stoicism.

Martial artists of the present day have become accustomed to sword demonstrations intended to display both the skill of the swordsman and the sharpness of his blade. For example, slicing a melon in half while it is resting on the body of a volunteer. English maisters of old also enjoyed demonstrating their skill in similar manner. One such feat being to slice an apple in half while it was resting on the palm of a brave helper. Another interesting display, designed to show the superb cutting quality of the blade, was to cut a broom stick in half while it was balanced across two wine glasses, without, of course, breaking the glasses. Also, in impressive imitation of Prince Offa, to slice a suspended beef carcass in half with one blow of a sword.[7]

Before moving on to the methods of the maisters it should be pointed out that English martial arts were not the sole preserve of men. An example of this has been handed down to us from the time of Henry VIII.[8] It again concerns Long Meg who was employed as a servant at The Eagle in Westminster. One of her customers was a knight by the name of Sir James of Castille (a Spanish knight). It would appear that Sir James was in love with Long Meg. However, his advances were declined by her on the grounds that she loved another. Upon receiving this news the distraught knight declared that if he knew who loved Long Meg he would "runne him thorow with his Rapier". This declaration gave Meg's fun loving mistress the idea to play a prank upon the unsuspecting knight. First she had Meg dress up in men's clothing and wait in the nearby St. George's field. Meanwhile she went to Sir James and told him that she had been insulted and that the offender was waiting in the said St. George's field. The unsuspecting but gallant knight immediately swore to punish the man in question. Accordingly he presented himself to the offender and challenged 'him' to a duel. Long Meg, armed with a sword and buckler, accepted the challenge and accordingly the two antagonists set to. Meg wounded the knight in his hand and demanded, and received, his surrender. At a later date, after Sir James had recounted the tale of his defeat at the hands of an English swordsman, it was revealed to him that his opponent had been Long Meg. A cruel jest perhaps, but one which Sir James accepted with grace and gallantry.

---

[7] J. M. Waite, *Lessons in Sabre, Singlestick, Bayonet, and Sword Feats.*
[8] Capt. A. Hutton, *The Sword and the Centuries.*

5 THE QUARTERSTAFF

Sticks and stones, as the old English rhyme suggests, are capable of breaking bones. They are also readily available, consequently they were mankind's earliest weapons and, as might be expected, martial arts systems the world over contain stick fighting methods within their curriculum. One of the 'sticks' used in the English system is the quarterstaff, also variously known as; club, cudgel, stave, staff, shortstaff, balstaff, balkstaff and tipstaff.

The quarterstaff, for obvious reasons, has always been portrayed as a peasant's weapon. It wasn't unknown, however, for people from the higher classes to express pride in their ability with this 'most noble weapon'. It appears to have been most commonly cut from ash or oak, although by the nineteenth century bamboo was also being used. Better quality staffs were often tipped, or shod, at each end with metal. As for its length, contemporary literature shows that the chosen dimensions of the weapon varied enormously. Wylde, Swetnam, Silver, Winn, and McCarthy, variously recommended lengths between seven and nine feet. On the other hand, contemporary illustrations of stage-gladiators and tipstaffs[1], if drawn to scale, show them holding staffs of around six feet in length.

Silver, in talking of military usage, recommended a method by which people could establish the length best suited to their stature:

> ...you shall stand upright, holding the staff upright close to your body with your left hand, reaching with your right hand your staffe as high as you can, and then allow to that length a space to set both your hands when you come to fight, wherein you may conveniently strike, thrust and ward, and that is your just length to be made according to your stature. And this note, that those lengths will commonly fall out to be eight or nine foot long,...

Such lengths are understandable when one considers those of the weapons against which the quarterstaff might be pitched on the battlefield; the two hand

---

[1] Tipstaffs were sheriff's officers who took their name from the weapon with which they were armed, that is to say a metal-tipped quarterstaff, otherwise known as a tipstaff.

sword, blackbill, and battle-axe, averaged between five and six feet in length. The longstaff could be upwards of twelve feet, while lengths of sixteen or eighteen feet were not unknown for the pike. These measurements are not in any way to be accepted as standard but they convey the danger of facing such weapons with a staff below the 'just length'. To highlight this point we can do no better than to consider again the teachings of Silver:

> If they should be shorter, then the long staffe, Morris Pike, and such like weapons over and above the perfect length, should have great vantage against them, because he [that uses them] may come boldly and safe without anie guard or ward to the place where he may thrust home, and at everie thrust put him in danger of his life: but if these weapons [quarterstaff etc.] be of their perfect lengths then can the long staffe, the Morris Pike, or anie other longer weapon ly no where in true space, but shall be still within compasse of the crosse and uncrosse, whereby he may safely passe home to the place, where he may strike or thrust him that hath the long weapon, in the head, face, or body at his pleasure…
>
> Now for the vantage of the short Staffe against the Sword & Buckler, Sword and Target, Two Hand Sword, Single Sword, Sword and Dagger, or Rapier and Poiniard, there is no great question to be made in anie of these weapons: whensoever anie blow or thrust shall be strongly made with the staffe, they are ever in a false place, in the carriage of the wards, for if at any of these six weapons he carrie his ward high and strong for his head, as of necessitie he must carie it verie high, otherwise it will be too weake to defend a blow being strongly made at the head, then will his space be too wide, in due time to break the thrust from his bodie. Againe if he carie his ward lower, thereby to be in equall space for readinesse to break both blow and thrust, then in that place his ward is too low, and too weake to defend the blow of the staffe: for the blow being strongly made at the head upon that ward, will beate downe the ward and his head together, and put him in great danger of his life…
>
> Yet againe for the short staffe: the short staffe hath the advantage against the Battel-axe, blacke-bill, or halbard, the short staffe hath the vantage, by reason of the nimbleness and length: he will strike and thrust freely, and in better and swifter time than can the Battel-axe, Black-bill, or Halbard: and by reason of his judgement, distance and time, fight safe…

Most people's knowledge of quarterstaff fighting is derived from fight scenes contained in period film and television productions. Such celluloid battles, though usually superb demonstrations of choreographic expertise and thespian ability, are not always based on traditional military methods. This shortcoming is, perhaps, understandable given the difficulty of peering into the shadows cast by Father Time. Further problems arise when we attempt to strip away the veneer laid on the art as a consequence of its shift into the sporting arena.

In this context it might be timely to consider the stage-gladiators' use of this weapon since they were responsible, in part at least, for the trend away from dangerous military techniques. A major reason for this change of martial emphasis was that they were professional sportsmen whose aim was victory, however painful, rather than the death of their opponents. This meant modifying methods and techniques so that the blows and targets used were less dangerous than the battlefield versions from which they originated. A further, though perhaps lesser, influence upon their methods would have been the constraints placed upon movement and tactics by the limited size of the raised platform upon which they fought. In engaging in sporting combat the stage-gladiators were merely following ancient custom. However, since the staff was, by their time, losing its military value their usage of the weapon came to be seen as normal.

Once embarked upon, the evolution brought about by sporting usage gathered apace. In the case of the quarterstaff, competitive fighting had reached its zenith by the end of the nineteenth century, though it lingered on into the early 1900's. By this time the weapon had long been militarily obsolete but it was still valued as a manly sport with good character building qualities. Illustrations of this period show staffmen dressed in padded helmets, face guards, fencing jackets, gauntlets, and cricket pads, hence removing it even further from the reality of life and death conflict.

The differences between battlefield and sporting usage of the quarterstaff are little short of astounding. Staff fighters of the sporting arena came to rely more and more upon methods based upon halfstaffing. That is to say when half the staff's length is held between the hands and the hands themselves are positioned equidistant from each end of the staff. This method results in the staffman standing very much closer to his opponent than would be the case in quarterstaffing. When halfstaffing, the butt (hinder end) of the staff is used as frequently as the 'tip'; and thrusts are usually 'put aside' (warded) with the 'myds' (middle) of the staff. Whereas in quarterstaffing the butt would only be used when one of the protagonists has succeeded in getting to close quarters, whilst thrusts would almost always be put aside with the foremost part of the staff. Thrusts were considered to be rather dangerous for competition fighting and were used less and less as time went on. Though, in any case, their frequency of use in the sporting version never matched that in the military system.

Military conflict required that a quarter of the length of the staff be held between the hands. The rear hand was positioned close to the butt of the staff while its tip was pointed forward. This meant that, with an eight or nine foot staff, there would be between five and six feet of staff between the foremost hand of the user and the nearest part of the opponent's weapon. Clearly this was to be preferred to the halfstaff grip which would place the user's hands within range of the opposing weapon. It doesn't take much imagination to realise that the halfstaff grip would have placed the user in grave danger when facing weapons such as the battle-axe or blackbill. Whereas when the quarterstaff stance was used the staffman was able to safely keep wielders of such weapons at bay. Unfortunately it is invariably halfstaffing that is shown on film and television. This is a great shame because quarterstaffing is a skilful and devastating art that is, at the least, as effective as its Oriental equivalents. It is indicative of the manner in which the weapon was most commonly used that it came to be known as the quarterstaff rather than the halfstaff.

Silver's confidence in this weapon led him to claim, not unjustly as will shortly be seen, that a man armed with the quarterstaff could defeat two men armed with sword and dagger. He justified his belief in the following manner:

> ...you shall plainely see, that whensoever anie of the Sword & Dagger men, Rapier and Poiniard men shall break his distance, or suffer the Staffe-man to breake his, that man which did first breake his distance, or suffer the distance to be won against him, is presently in danger of death. And this canot in reason be denied, because the distance appertaining to the Staffe-man either to keepe or breake, standeth upon the moving of one large pace alwayes at the most, both for his offence or safety. The other two in the breach of their distance to offend the Staffe-man have always foure at the least therein they fall too great in number with their feet, and too short in distance to offend the Staffe-man...

> But if the Sword and Dagger-men will in the time that they be before him... labor with all heed & diligence to be both or one of them behind him, that troubleth the Staffe-man nothing at all, for in that very time when he findeth them past the middle part of the circle, he presently turneth, by the which he naturally set himselfe as it were in a triangle, and both the sword and dagger-men, shall thereby stand both before him in true distance of three paces, from offending of him at the least, as at the first they did. And take this for a true ground, there is no man able to ward a sound blow with the Sword and Dagger, nor Rapier, Poiniard, and Gantlet [gauntlet], being strongly made at the head, with the Staffe, and run in withall, the force of both hands is such, being in his full motion and course, that although the other do carie his ward high and strong with both handes, yet his feete being moving from the ground, the great force of the [staffman's] blow will strike him with his ward, and all downe flat to the ground [even if the swordsman blocks strongly if he tries to close in at the

66

same time the force of the staff will knock him to the ground]. But if he [the swordsman] stands fast with his feete, he may with both weapons together, strongly defend his head from the blow but then you are sufficiently instructed, the [staffman's] thrust being presently made after the blow full at the bodie, it is impossible in due time to breake it, by reason of the largenesse of his [the swordsman's] space. [it would take too long for the swordsman to lower his weapons to be able to ward the staffman's second attack].

Silver's faith in the quarterstaff was shared by other maisters, one of them being Wylde who proclaimed, rather succinctly, the following:

...for a man that rightly understands it, may bid defiance and laugh at any other weapon...

The well reasoned dissertation of Silver compels us to accept the military logic of cutting staffs to the lengths recommended by him and the other maisters. But this begs the question, why were staffs as short as six feet used? Perhaps that query can be answered thus; away from the battlefield, in what we may term non-military usage, the staffman was unlikely to come up against such formidable implements as the pike or battle-axe. If drawn into a street brawl he was far more likely to be fighting against 'civilian' weapons such as the sword, sword and buckler, or the quarterstaff itself. In such circumstances staffs of the shorter length would be more than adequate. Similar reasoning can be applied to the staffs used by stage-gladiators, inasmuch as they invariably competed against like weapons. That is to say, sword against sword, staff against staff, and so on. In the latter instance they could fight with much shorter staffs and still retain martial equality. Indeed, such equality was a vital prerequisite of sporting combat.

The information presented so far, suggests that the quarterstaff is a weapon par excellence, but what evidence apart from old poems and the like, do we have that its lethal efficiency is that promised by the maisters of defence? The main source of evidence is not to be found in military legend but in the dusty realms of legal documentation. Court records from various parts of England furnish evidence that countless deaths were caused by the use of the quarterstaff in social disputes. However, such confrontations were not necessarily always between equally armed, equally proficient fighters. How would a trained staff fighter fare against a determined battle-hardened soldier in a life or death situation? It is a question that, thanks to the exploits of an English sailor by the name of Richard Peeke[2], we are able to answer.

---

[2] *Three to One* by Richard Peeke

In the year 1625 England and Spain were at war and Peeke was serving in an English naval squadron, under the command of the Earl of Essex, which was attacking a Spanish coastal stronghold. After heavy and accurate bombardment the English captured the fortress, whereupon the, sent forces ashore to carry the attack inland. In the wake of the English landings sailors were sent ashore to forage for food. Richard Peeke, of Tavistock in Devon, was among them. Unwisely he foraged alone and paid the price for his mistake when he was attacked by a patrol of Spanish musketeers. After a furious fight, during which Peeke was wounded twice, he was captured and taken in chains to Cales (Cadiz). From there he was transferred to Xeres where he was put on trial.

Present at his trial, which in reality was a military interrogation, were four dukes, four marquesses, and four earls. After much questioning Peeke was asked if he thought that the Spanish soldiers present would prove such 'hennes' as the English when they landed in England the following year.

"No", replied Peeke, "they would prove to be pullets or chickens."

Peeke's insolent reply brought forth an angry response from the Spaniards.

"Darst thou then (quoth Duke Medyna, with a brow half angry) fight with one of these Spanish pullets."

Peeke replied that,

"...hee was unworthy the Name of an English Man, that should refuse to fight with one Man of any Nation whatsoever."

At this Peeke's chains and shackles were removed and a space was created for him to fight a Spanish champion by the name of Tiago. Both were armed with rapier and poniard (a type of dagger). The ensuing fight continued for some time before Peeke, using the guard of the poniard, trapped the blade of Tiago's rapier and simultaneously swept the Spaniard's feet from under him.[3] Peeke's rapier, held to the throat of senór Tiago brought forth the necessary capitulation. Spanish pride had been sorely wounded and it was demanded of Peeke whether he would be willing to fight another Spaniard. Peeke replied in the affirmative provided that he was allowed to fight with:

"...mine Owne Countrey Weapon, called the Quarter-staffe."

Upon this remark the Spanish unscrewed the head from a halberd to create a makeshift quarterstaff. Armed with the weapon of his choice Peeke stood ready

---

[3] The leg-sweep was a favoured technique of English martial artists.

to meet his next challenger. However the Spanish were clearly no longer so confident in the prowess of their soldiers for, to Peeke's consternation, two swordsmen stepped forward to fight him. Peeke sarcastically asked if more would join them. The Duke Medyna asked how many he desired to fight.

"Any number under sixe", replied Peeke.

The Duke smiled scornfully and beckoned a third man to join the original two. Peeke and the rapier men warily traversed each other, all the while thrusting and warding, till finally Peeke gambled on an all-out attack. His first blow left one of his adversaries dead and his subsequent blows left the other two injured and disarmed. No doubt they also left the Spanish seriously questioning the wisdom of their invasion plans.

Peeke's feat so impressed his Spanish captors that they released him and granted him safe conduct to England.

6 THE BILL

Some idea of the military importance of the bill[1] may be gained by considering that it stars alongside the bow in the ancient English rallying-cry of 'Bows and Bills!'. That the bill should be associated in this manner with the devastatingly effective longbow speaks volumes for its military credentials. Quite clearly it was a favoured item of the Englishman's arsenal and its use has been recorded since Anglo-Saxon times.

The weapon wasn't peculiar to the English, being used in countries as far flung as Turkey and Iceland. The latter nation giving us the legend of 'Gunnar's' bill which was said to sing before battle. However, it does seem that the English made more use of it than most nations. It is not difficult to understand their appreciation of the bill because it was near to being the ideal close quarters weapon. A man armed with it could, for example, confidently oppose those carrying swords or pikes. He could even face the terrifying battleaxe knowing that his own weapon was capable of like carnage. Finally, and perhaps most importantly, he was more than capable of resisting knights and men-at-arms, as the following account by Wace proves:

> There was a French soldier of noble mien, who sat his horse gallantly. He spied two English-men who were also carrying themselves boldly. They were men of great worth and had become companions in arms, and fought together, the one protecting the other. They bore two long and broad bills, and did great mischief to the Normans, killing both horses and men...

The battle of Flodden (September 1513) fought between the English (commanded by the Earl of Surrey) and the Scottish (commanded by King James IV), is, from a military viewpoint, a fine example of this weapon's combat efficiency. The

---

[1] The term *bill* (Old English *bil*) means 'cutting tool' and therefore may apply to a range of implements rather than to a specific type. However, the agricultural implement was also known as a billhook, that is to say a cutting hook, and in this context it is possible to regard the term bill as an abbreviation referring to a weapon/blade of a particular design. In any case the term is now generally taken to refer to the type of weapon discussed in this chapter.

Scots, who had been trained in the methods of the *Landknechts*[2], were formed up in five huge battalions in the manner of the Swiss[3]. Fortescue, in his *History of the British Army,* tells us that the English fielded an army of 26,000 against a Scottish force of 40,000. Despite outnumbering the English so heavily the Scots were to suffer a devastating defeat during which 10,000 of their men, including King James himself, were to lose their lives. Many of the dead Scots were the victims of the clothyard arrows which were loosed at them with horrific accuracy by the English bowmen. However, at close quarters the damage was wrought by billmen whose weapons proved to be infinitely superior to the pikes of their foe.

The bill was one of the most versatile close-combat weapons ever used, a quality that fitted well with the highly developed fighting skills of the English. A favourite tactic of billmen was to hack off the heads of the pikes opposing them, which left the pikemen holding long useless staffs. Such a tactic had long been popular with the English, as proved by the words of Wace when writing of the Battle of Hastings (1066):

> And now might be heard the loud clang and cry of battle, and the clashing of lances. The English stood firm in their barricades, and shivered the [enemies] lances, beating them into pieces with their bills.

The importance of this pole-arm is further underlined by a 1547 Tower of London inventory of arms which showed that the best part of 7,000 bills were held in its armoury. Perhaps this figure is not overly impressive when compared with the massive firepower of modern armies but it assumes due respect when set within the context of contemporary conflict. As an example it is worth considering the following breakdown of forces fielded by the English at Formigny (France) on the 15th April, 1450. Out of a total number of 4,500 English troops, 2,000 were longbowmen, a few hundred were men-at-arms, and the rest were billmen. In other words, the royal armoury held enough bills to equip three contemporary armies.

A report about English military methods written in 1551 by Daniel Barbaro, the Venetian ambassador to the English court, contained a description of the type of bill with which the sixteenth century English warrior would have been familiar:

---

[3] The Swiss were renowned as Europe's leading pike fighters, though it is arguable that, at a later date, the German *Landknechts* were just as good.

[2] *Landknechts* means servants of the land and was the term applied to professional German troops whose methods and tactics were similar to those of the Swiss. They fought with a variety of weapons of which the pike was the most important.

The infantry is formed of taller men and divided into four sorts. The first is of archers, who abound in England and are very excellent, both by nature and from practise, so that the archers alone have often been seen to rout armies of 30,000 men. The second is of bill-men, their weapon being a short, thick staff, with an iron [blade] like a peasant's hedging bill, but much thicker and heavier than what is used in the Venetian territories. With this they strike so violently as to unhorse the cavalry; and it is made short because they like close quarters.

Barbaro's observations about the weight and length of English bills are borne out by the words of Silver who, when writing about the black bill, mentions that they:

> …may not well be used much longer, because of their weights: and being weapons for the warres or battells when men are joyned close together, may thrust and strike sound blowes with great force both strong and quicke.

Yet the bill, which had served the English so well, was to receive short shrift from the powers that be. In 1596 the Crown issued instructions that all local forces in England should replace the bill with the pike, an edict which must have dismayed Sir Roger Williams whose book, *A Briefe Discourse Of Warre* (published in 1590) strongly commended the use of the bill.

> I persuade myself that there ought to be amongst one thousand pikes, 200. short weapons, as Holberts or Bills; but the Bills must bee of good stuffe, not like our common browne Bills, which are lightlie [commonly] for the most part all yron, with a little steele or none at all; but they ought to bee made of good yron and steele, with long strong pikes at the least of 12. inches long, armed with yron to the midds of the staffe, like the Holberts; for example, like unto those which the Earle of Leicester, and Sir William Pelham had in the Low Countries for their guards; being made thus, no doubt but it is a necessarie weapon to guard ensignes in the field, Trenches or Townes, and a good weapon to execute…

Despite the ruling of 1596 the bill was to linger on as a weapon of the people for generations to come. It did in fact appear to have been in official military use as late as 1681 when it was known to have formed part of the armoury of Britain's Tangier garrison.

An enormous variety of bills were produced, many of which, such as those pictured overleaf, survive in collections. Unfortunately it is not a weapon which inspired much literary attention, so it is not possible, with any degree of confidence,

Figure 3 15th century English Bill (left) and 18th century English Hedging Bill Hedging Bill photo: with thanks to the Histrionix Living History Group

to accurately match names to designs. The names which attract attention in a martial context are: forest bill, hedging bill, black bill, and brown bill.

At least, we now know that the brown bill was common and that it was usually made of iron. If we then assume a link between the 'thicker and heavier' blades described by Barbaro and the 'good yron and steele' bills recommended by Sir Roger it is possible that both of them were discussing the same, or at least similar, weapon, that is to say a military version of the ferrous agricultural implement. Leading on from this is the possibility that the iron and steel bills inferred by Sir Roger were the black bills mentioned by Silver. In other words it is possible that the brown bill and black bill were named after the characteristics of the materials from which they were manufactured and were not, necessarily, weapons of different design. Unfortunately such speculation, despite its convenience, is too fragile to assert with any confidence. Nonetheless, it is interesting to note that Grose, in his *Military Antiquities* (1786), states the same belief but bases it, in the case of the black bill, on a different reason:

> The black or, as it is sometimes called, the brown bill was a kind of halbert, the cutting part hooked like a woodsman's bill, from the back of which projected a spike, and another at the head. The denomination of black or brown arose from its colour; the one from a black varnish with which this weapon was frequently covered, the other from its being often brown with rust.

The explanation may indeed be as simple as Grose tells us, he was after all a meticulous collector of information and one finds it hard to doubt his words. However, a foreign visitor to these climes recorded information which may do just that. Paul Hentzner in his *Travels in England* (1598), recounts, after a visit to the Tower of London armoury, that:

> Eight or nine men, employed by the year, are scarce sufficient to keep all the arms bright.

We know that the Tower of London armoury held almost 7,000 bills, and we may reasonably suppose that these bills were among the weapons kept 'bright' by a team of cleaners. Stored, varnished weapons would at most need dust wiping from them and would certainly not be bright if covered in black varnish. This is not to doubt the words of Grose, it is after all perfectly feasible that varnishing took place in his day, but that is not to say that his explanation was necessarily valid in earlier times. Nonetheless, there is little difference between his contention and that of the author that the brown bill and black bill were of the same design. The only difference being that the author believes the black bill was named after the colouring derived from its metallic content rather than varnish. As for the colouring of the brown bill there is complete agreement between both parties.

Similar problems present themselves in regard to the forest bill. Silver says that the length of a forest bill was between eight and nine feet long and that it was the only weapon which he considered to be equal to the quarterstaff. This suggests, bearing in mind the lightness of the quarterstaff, that the forest bill had a much lighter blade than its shorter cousins. This proposal fits well with Silver's admonition that the length of black bills; "may not be well used much longer, because of their weights". Such a supposition might also make sense when considering the normal use to which a forest bill would be put, though once again the fragility of such speculation must be underlined. However, despite the uncertainty concerning names and characteristics, it is beyond dispute that the bill was one of the most devastating close quarter weapons ever devised.

One further weapon which should be mentioned is the Welsh hook. Although little is known about this arm it is mentioned by Silver who seems to juxtapose its use with that of the forest bill. The problem of identifying the various types of bill pale into insignificance when attempting the like with the Welsh hook, or, as Silver describes it, the 'welche hooke'. Catalogues held at the Tower of London's Royal Armoury define the Welsh hook as a gisarme. This would be a useful identification if it could be generally maintained but unfortunately it is difficult to find any two sources that agree as to the actual classification of the gisarme itself, it variously being described as a bill, partisan, double axe, curved sword, glaive, and so on. In the Statute of Winchester (1285) the gisarme is described as a weapon of the 'lower people' but a statute of King William of Scotland (1165-1214), describes it as a handbill. Such tantalizing confusion does not help us to relate this weapon to the Welsh hook.

Figure 4 Welsh hook

However, most of the designs alluded to above would not be suitable for the martial duties seemingly ascribed to the Welsh hook by Silver. Fortunately, *The Book of Days*, by R. Chambers (1863), contains a woodcut (dated 1749) picturing the goods and chattels of one William Morgan. One of the items depicted is a Welsh hook, a replica is shown above. The picture, if representative, would seem to distance the Welsh hook from all but one of the definitions of the gisarme. That exception being the bill, the generic territory of which would seem to be the proper home of the Welsh hook.

7   Bare-Fist Fighting

The theory of evolution holds that mankind developed from the ape family, or at least from an ape-like creature. This being so it comes as no surprise that human beings have inherited certain ape-like traits, such as striking with the clenched fist. For that matter, since our furry relatives sometimes make use of sticks and stones when fighting we must apply the same Darwinian logic when considering mankind's use of other weapons.

In view of the above it would be extremely unwise for any nation to claim seniority in the martial arts hierarchy unless of course they can prove that their particular branch of the human family was the first to evolve from the 'missing link'. That being said, it cannot be denied that some nations have unarmed combat traditions of great antiquity, The Greeks, for example, included boxing in the ancient Olympics as early as 688BC. From the land of the Pharaohs comes evidence that the ancient Egyptians practised a system of unarmed combat six thousand years ago. Twelve hundred years before Bhodidharma (the oft supposed founder of kung fu) set foot in the now famous Shao-lin temple, the Celts of the Halstatt culture were decorating their pottery with boxing scenes. Over a millennium later, but still a century ahead of Bhodidharma, the industrious quill of Ammianus Marcellinus (c. AD. 400) recorded that:

> Almost all the Gauls are of tall stature, fair and ruddy, terrible for the fierceness of their eyes, fond of quarrelling, and of overbearing insolence. In fact a whole band of foreigners will be unable to cope with one of them in a fight, if he calls in his wife, stronger than he by far and with flashing eyes; least of all when she swells her neck and gnashes her teeth, and poising her huge white arms, begins to rain blows mingled with kicks, like shots discharged by the twisted cords of a catapult.

We know of the systems and skills mentioned above because the peoples in question had an early written tradition or were governed by, or known to, those with such a tradition. Many other peoples, including Northern Europeans, had strong oral traditions; that is to say that knowledge was committed to the cultural memory rather than to parchment. It would be easy to mistakenly believe that cultures with oral traditions were less sophisticated than those with written traditions. Of course, in many cases this was true, however there were sagacious nations that entrusted their wisdom to the collective mind in the belief that this better preserved their social unity and culture. However, the oral tradition ultimately proved to be vulnerable and when those oral societies ceased to exist vast amounts of knowledge known to them was lost. So it comes as no surprise that we are unable to date the emergence of many of our European martial arts systems as accurately as some of those emanating from the Near and Far East. Nevertheless it is not unreasonable to date the beginnings of such arts from the time when the nations that created them came into existence rather than from when the arts were first recorded. Of course, if we follow this line of reasoning to its conclusion we must ultimately argue such styles back to their common Indo-European origins; to a time, as intimated, before the invention of writing because, as Marston wrote:

> A Master of Fence is more honourable than a M^r. of art; for good fighting was before good writing.

The logic of Marston's hypothesis is not to be denied, nor is the fact that the Germanic peoples, Engle (English) included, were capable of 'good fighting' long before 'good writing' recorded the technical details of their martial skills.

Whatever the antiquity of English martial arts the fact remains that we are unaware of the precise methodology of early English fighting systems. There are, however, certain factors which can be confidently ascertained; such as knowing that the Anglo-Saxon *folcwiga* (warrior) considered skills in unarmed combat a vital part of *wigræden* (way of warfare), an attitude shared by English warrior kings. King Alfred the Great, for instance, was reputed to be as skilled at boxing and wrestling as he was at weaponed fighting. Indeed, according to Pierce the Elder, Alfred was at pains to enrich his warriors with the same skills:

> ...in recurring to the times of the immortal Alfred, according to ancient authorities, we shall find, that wrestling and boxing formed a part of the manual exercise of the soldiers at that distant period.

To the modern mind the idea of members of a royal family effecting a perfect cross-buttock[1], or throwing a vicious right hook might seem somewhat novel, but Germanic chroniclers assure us that this was indeed the case. According to Saxo, Hother (adopted son of Gewar, king of Norway) was unequalled in boxing and wrestling. He further informs us that Starkad killed an enemy warrior with a

---

[1] A wrestling throw commonly used in bare-fist fighting.

single blow of his fist. It was a royal practice that died hard and many are the references to pugilistic skills of English kings. King Richard III, for example, was said by Egan to have been:

> …particularly distinguished with a clenched fist, when opposed to an antagonist, by the extreme potency of his arm.

The fighting prowess of King Edward was such that there are fourteenth century tales telling of his ability to hold his own at wrestling and fisticuffs with the great Robin Hood himself.[2]

In military terms the importance of unarmed combat systems declined in inverse proportion to the increased effectiveness of projectile weaponry. The survival of such systems came to depend on non-military factors such as the need for personal self-defence. As the bearing of arms by civilians declined so the importance of traditional unarmed combat skills grew. Another factor that helped to preserve and promote such skills was the popularity of fighting as a form of entertainment. Although similar developments took place in other countries it was in England that modern Western boxing was born.

To explain why this happened it is necessary to consider a rather curious convention; this being that for the greater part of her existence England had no standing army and because of that, as explained in the opening chapter, England's monarchs had to rely on the civilian population for the defence of the realm. The English took such responsibilities seriously and considered it their duty to be skilled in the military arts. Nor, if we take note of contemporary writings, did they regard this duty as being at all onerous. Their love of combat, whether as participant or spectator became something of a byword in foreign parts. This eager determination to answer the call of duty was good news for the 'Scholes of Fence' and their proprietors who happily catered for the patriotic wishes of their customers. Those who didn't attend the schools often proved their affinity to martial arts by attending the public staging of challenges and prizes. These performances, with their colourful ceremony and exciting displays were regarded as excellent distractions by the large crowds that turned out to witness them.

When the traditional maisters of defence disappeared from the scene their events were 'hijacked' by the 'stage-gladiators' who took their place following the Restoration.[3] As well as being skilled martial artists such people were often consummate businessmen who were not slow to cash in on an activity that Zacharias von Uffenbach described as, 'a truly English amusement'. Thus the

---

[2] As Bryant points out in his book, *The Age of Chivalry*, it is not known which of the three Angevin Edwards, whose dynasty lasted from 1272 to 1377, is being referred to.

[3] The restoration of King Charles II on 29th May, 1660.

mechanisms and the stimulus for boxing to attain commercial viability in England was already in place when skilled boxers (or those who thought themselves to be so) presented themselves to the entrepreneurs of the day eager to share the purses that were going the way of the weapon wielders. It is interesting to note that the stage-gladiators were not the first martial entertainers. Centuries before they arrived on the scene skilled martial artists, in collaboration with minstrels, were in demand to act out fight scenes at fairs, feasts, revels, and the like.

But what of the art itself? Without delving too deeply into the technical side of bare-fist fighting, which will be dealt with later, it is possible to furnish an overall picture of its content. In its early days English bare-fist fighting included throws, locks, sweeps, and kicks. That the 'English fight' did not rely on the fist alone is evidenced by early English manuscript illustrations[4] depicting fighting methods that would not look out of place in a kung fu or jiu-jitsu syllabus. In fact when the full scope of English unarmed combat is appreciated it becomes clear that its title is something of a misnomer as it fails to take into account all of the aspects of the art. Yet the expression remains a convenient one to use, for it has long since claimed a place in the English language and in using it, we are taking no greater licence than either the Chinese, who use such terms as 'ch'uan-shu' (the art of the fist) or the Japanese, who term their art 'karate' (empty hand fighting), when it is well known that neither system relies purely on hand techniques.

Over the centuries various references have been made to English unarmed combat but they are usually of little technical use. Practical information only begins to emerge when the popularity of the art made books a viable commercial proposition. This, to all intents and purposes, came after boxers took to the gladiatorial stage. The earliest known journalistic reference to a fistic prize-fight seems to have been a short article carried in the Protestant Mercury, a newspaper which, on the 12th January 1681, reported the following event:

> Yesterday (11th) a match of boxing was performed before his grace the Duke of Albermarle between the Duke's footman and a butcher. The latter won the prize as he hath done many before, being accounted though but a little man, the best at that exercise in England.

This report suggests that prize-fights were already quite common by the latter part of the seventeenth century. There is even the suggestion of an English championship, albeit unofficial, in that the butcher was recognised as the best fighter in England. Clearly, bare-fist fighting was on its way to popular acclaim and by the end of the same century it had become big business. This was witnessed by the growing number of public exhibitions, such as the one held at the Theatre Royal in London's Salisbury Square in 1698. Given this type of public support

---

[4] The fourteenth century *Queen Mary's Psalter*, Plate 197 (ff167–168).

and commercial backing it wasn't long before bare-fist fighting began to rival weapon fighting in the affections of the public.

The men responsible for teaching, developing, and displaying the fistic arts were a singular breed. Tough and courageous to an extent which bordered on foolhardiness. These men were, without question, the equal of any master produced by the martial schools of Asia (as indeed were their predecessors). These new maisters, or stage-gladiators, were people who, in order to earn their living, regularly proved their skill and courage in public trials of combat. In this they were continuing the tradition of their martial forbears, the maisters of fence. It is to one of these stage-gladiators, James Figg, that we now turn our attention.

In discussing James Figg we are undoubtedly turning the literary spotlight upon one of the greatest martial artists of all time. A man who strode through the martial arts world like a colossus. James Figg fought almost three hundred fights with fists and weapons and lost only once, a defeat which he very soon avenged. Whilst it is true that Figg fought mostly with weapons he was nevertheless a superb boxer and well recognised as such. It has to be pointed out that when boxing, these men fought without gloves, and that choking, throwing, and kicking (even when the man was down) were all, at that time, allowed. In armed combat they fought with weapons that were neither rebated nor padded and horrific injuries and deaths could and did occur. However, for the time being, it is with Figg's boxing skills that we are concerned. Born at Thame, in Oxfordshire, Figg held the English boxing title from 1719 until his death in 1734. During his lifetime Figg's abilities brought him the adoration of the masses and the patronage of the rich and famous. Amongst them such dignitaries as King George II, the writer Jonathan Swift, the poet Alexander Pope, and the artist William Hogarth. One might almost consider that Figg was England's first sporting superstar.

Figg proved to have amazing business acumen. His interests ranged from a boxing booth in London's famous Southwark Fair to his own martial arts academy in Oxford Road. He also became a fight promoter and staged an international contest between Tito Alberto di Carni and an Englishman named Bob Whittaker. Carni, who fought under the name of 'The Venetian Gondolier', was by all accounts a huge, powerful man famous for the strength of his punching rather than his pugilistic skills. Figg, when warned of Carni's extraordinary strength and propensity for breaking jaws, laughed heartily and replied:

> I do not know master, but he may break one of his own countrymen's jaw-bones with his fist, but I will bring him a man, and he shall not break his jaw-bone with a sledgehammer.

Whittaker, the man in whom Figg placed so much faith, was not regarded as being a particularly good boxer but he was renowned for two things; his expert ability at throwing people and his courage and endurance (bottom).

One can imagine the excitement pervading the air on the evening of the fight as rival fans shouted support for their respective heroes. One can also imagine English voices being shocked into silence when the first punch of the contest was thrown, for it was a Venetian punch and it landed on the hapless Whittaker's jaw to send him crashing several feet to the ground from the raised platform on which they fought. Venetian ecstasy, however, was short lived for Whittaker was tough, very tough, he had to be just to survive the training in English boxing. Accordingly Whittaker leapt back on to the platform and resumed the fray. The next punch was again Venetian and it was again aimed at the jaw. This time however it didn't connect because Whittaker slipped the punch and landed his own blow on Carni's solar plexus. The effect was stupendous, for the giant Venetian collapsed as if pole-axed. The shock must have been almost as bad as the pain, because it was not a punch that he had experienced before, it being a speciality of English boxing. Carni, who had boasted that he would, "Take the shine out of Englishmen", was about to regret his words as Egan's account makes plain:

> Bob now punished his man in fine style, drove the Venetian all over the stage and soon gave him a leveller.
> In the cause of a few rounds the conceit was so taken out of him that he lost all guard of his person and was compelled to give in.

This early international contest serves well to illustrate the differences that had developed between English boxing and the often rudimentary skills displayed by foreign entrants to the English 'ring'. It also serves to reveal the vast gulf in ability between the best that Venice had to offer when compared to the English product. This is highlighted by the fact that when the brave Whittaker fought Nathaniel Peartree a week later he was defeated in only six minutes.

The toughness displayed by Whittaker was more than pure instinct or determination, it was also empirical, instilled by the hard training methods of Figg and his contemporaries. Just as modern boxers learn to 'take a punch', so their ancestors learned to take punishment in the harsh and merciless martial academies of the day. The words of one of Figg's students, Captain John Godfrey, will serve to illustrate further the methods of Figg and his peers:

> I have purchased my knowledge with many a broken head[lacerations] and bruises on every part of me. I chose to go mostly to Figg and exercise with him, partly because I knew him to be the ablest master and partly, as he was of a rugged temper and would spare no man, high or low who took up a stick against him.

However, it must not be imagined that Figg or his ilk were hard taskmasters purely for the sake of brutality, for their methods were simply a reflection of a society that was tough and unrelenting to a degree that we today are unable to comprehend. In fairness to Figg it must be pointed out that his uncompromising attitude was backed up by superlative skills. For confirmation of this we need only return to the words of Godfrey who described Figg thus:

> Figg was the Atlas of the Sword, and may he remain the gladiating Statue! In him, Strength, Resolution, and unparallel'd Judgement conspired to form a matchless Master. There was a majesty shone in his Countenance, and blazed in all his actions, beyond all I ever saw. His right leg bold and firm, and his left which could hardly ever be disturbed, gave him the surprising Advantage already proved, and struck his Adversary with Despair and Panic. He had that peculiar way of stepping in, I spoke of, in a Parry; he knew his Arm and its just time of moving, put a firm Faith in that and never let his Adversary escape his Parry. He was just as much a great MASTER, than any other I ever saw, as he was a greater Judge of Time and Measure. Figg is the most perfect example of self-defence of his day. Seconded by his strength and temper, his skill renders him invincible.

Short though this eulogy is, it was written by a man who was himself a martial artist of no mean repute. The words therefore give us a glimpse of some of the things which made James Figg a master martial artist. A man, by all accounts, of skill, courage, honour, and integrity. A true and worthy descendant of the maisters of fence and a vigorous guardian of the spirit of English martial arts.

It is now time to move onto the man who was destined to follow James Figg onto the patriarchal pedestal of English bare-fist fighting. That man was Jack Broughton (1704–1789) and, like Figg, he was skilled with stick and sword as well as with fists. However it was mainly for his contributions to boxing that Broughton was to achieve well deserved fame. English champion from 1740 to 1750 he is considered by many to be the 'Father' of boxing as we know it today. Broughton was a fighter of immense skill and courage who, like Figg before him, must be recognised as one of the all time greats. For confirmation of this we can look at the writings of Pierce Egan who said of Broughton the following:

> Broughton, like all great masters, generally exhibited something new in every performance; and those pugilists who had witnessed his contests, and afterwards entered the lists against him, expecting to find that he would fight upon the old suit, were most terribly deceived; as contrary to most other boxers, he did not depend upon any particular blow, although he was distinguished for giving some remarkable hits, which were scarcely ever forgotten. Broughton, when necessary in the conflict, by putting in his stomach blow, has often decided the battle; and his lunge under the

ear generally produced terrible consequences to his opponent. The eye of Broughton was most lively and acute, soon perceiving the weakness of any adversary; and his arm, keeping pace with that valuable assistant, protected him from the most destructive blows; and his quick penetration made him always aware of any direct intent pursued by his adversary, as immediately to render it futile and unavailing. His guard was considered so complete that his frame appeared as well secured as if in a fence. Uncommon strength and bottom often fell before him; and his expertness in the cross-buttock was great. His various attitudes were fine and impressive, and his countenance always animated and cheerful.

Broughton also came to the attention of Godfrey who remarked of him thus:

> Has he not all that others want, and all the best can have? Strength equal to what is human, Skill and Judgement equal to what can be acquired, undebauched Wind, and a bottom spirit, never to pronounce the word Enough. He fights the stick as well as most men, and understands a good deal of the Small-Sword. This practice has given him the Distinction of Time and Measure beyond the rest. He stops as regularly as the Swords-Man, and carries his Blows truely in the Line; he steps not back, distrusting of himself to stop a Blow, and piddle in the Return, with an Arm unaided by his Body, producing but a kind of flyflap Blows; such as the Pastry-Cooks use to beat those Insects from their Tarts and Cheesecakes. No-BROUGHTON steps bold and firmly in, bids a Welcome to the coming blow; receives it with his guardian Arm; then with a general Summons of his swelling Muscles, and his firm Body, seconding his Arm, and supplying it with all its weight, pours the Pile-driving Force upon his Man.

Praise indeed for the skills of a truly great martial artist, but his achievements didn't end there; in 1743 he introduced a code of rules which, with minor modifications, were to govern boxing until 1838, when they were superseded by the 'London Prize Ring Rules'.

It was this 'Code of Rules' implemented by Broughton which paved the way for the development of modern western boxing. The inherent effect of these rules was to steer bare-fist fighting away from its 'all-in' unarmed combat format by barring certain of the more dangerous methods, this in turn was to lead (eventually) to a purely fistic system. Such things as hitting or kicking a fallen opponent became illegal. Seizing an opponent by the ham or breeches was outlawed. Indeed the seizing of an opponent <u>anywhere</u> below the waist was banned. Even with Broughton's civilising modifications bare-fist fighting was still a very tough and dangerous system. The severity of the art led to many serious injuries and even deaths. In 1741 Broughton fought, and beat, George Stevenson, so badly did he injure his opponent in the forty minute contest that Stevenson died a few days later, causing the distressed Broughton to introduce his rules in an effort to prevent such a thing happening again.

Apart from making the art somewhat safer (many dangerous techniques were still allowed) his regulations also enhanced the art's respectability by, for example, promoting fair and impartial refereeing, and introducing provisions which guaranteed that fighters received a fair percentage of the gate money. From all of the aforementioned we can see that Broughton hugely deserves the fame and respect that he was accorded. However, he was to make one further contribution to the art, that being the introduction of padded gloves. Though one suspects that his farsightedness in this was related more to his financial future than to the future of boxing. For the use of these gloves, or mufflers as he called them, was designed to attract into his gym the richer, but perhaps more genteel upper classes of society who, quite sensibly, didn't relish suffering the broken jaws and noses that were common hazards in the training of those days. Proof of Broughton's reasoning can be seen in the wording of an advertisement which he placed in 1747:

> m^r Broughton proposes, with proper assistance, to open an Academy at his house in the Haymarket... where that truly British art [boxing] with all the various blows, stops, cross buttocks etc., incidental to the combatants will be fully taught and explained; and that persons of quality and distinction may not be debarred from entering into a course of these lectures they will be given with the utmost tenderness and regard to the delicacy of the frame and constitution of the pupil. For which reason mufflers are provided that will effectually secure them from the inconveniency of black eyes, broken jaws and bloody noses.

It should be pointed out that Broughton introduced gloves, or mufflers, purely as a training aid and that for a long time to come actual fights were still fought bare-fisted. Nonetheless the use of gloves in training became an accepted convention which paved the way for their use in contests.

Sadly the story of this great man did not end perfectly for he committed boxing's cardinal sin of having one fight too many. Losing his title to Jack Slack, alias the Norwich Butcher. Yet his one defeat cannot take away his many achievements and he retired into eventual dignity from the boxing scene. He died a wealthy man and such was his standing that even in death he was accorded one final accolade, a plaque being raised to his memory in the cloisters of Westminster Abbey.

With the advent of the none too reputable Slack bare-fist fighting suffered its first serious decline in popularity. Due in the main, or so it is thought, to fight-fixing which resulted in a series of mediocre fights and fighters. Happily a saviour was to arrive in the shape of a fighter named Tom Johnson (real name Tom Jackling). Bare-fist fighting owed a great debt to this fine fighter, for during the eight years that he held the title, his skill, courage, and integrity rescued the art from the corruption and public apathy which had engulfed it. The saviour of bare-fist fighting, if we may so describe Tom Johnson, finally lost his title to Big Ben Brain in a furiously fought eighteen round contest in 1791. The fight must have been particularly distressing for Brain because he suffered serious damage to his liver and consequently was never able to defend his title. Sadly, Brain was to die three years later as a result, so it seems, of the serious injuries suffered in his fight against Johnson.

Other good fighters came and went but the next major influence upon the art was one Daniel Mendoza. Born in London's East End in 1763 he was destined to become one of boxing's greats. Mendoza's contribution to bare-fist fighting was probably his style of combat. He was a small man, standing only 5ft 7ins tall and weighing about 12st. and, since in those days there were no weight divisions, there were often huge differences in size and weight. Accordingly Mendoza had to rely on guile rather than force. This he did by utilizing a comprehensive system of blocking and counter-punching. He was also renowned for switching his lead and stance, which had the effect of confusing his opponents and, when correctly timed, of adding power to his blows. It would be no exaggeration to say that Mendoza was the finest boxer since the days of Broughton and Figg. Perhaps the following sentiments expressed by an eighteenth century observer will give us an insight into Mendoza's methods:

> Mendoza is a pugilist better initiated in the theory of boxing than perhaps any of his contemporaries, and has produced some exceedingly expert pupils. In his manner there is more neatness than strength and, it has been said, more show than service; his blows are generally deficient in force but given with astonishing quickness, and he is allowed to strike oftener, and stop more dextrously, than any other man; he is extremely well formed in the breast and arms, but his loins are very weak; his wind is good, and he possesses excellent bottom.

Mendoza's career consisted of thirty-five fights. He won the title in 1791 and held it until 1795 when he lost it to Gentleman John Jackson. It should be pointed out that the title of Gentleman applied to Jackson's demeanour outside the ring rather than in it, his methods against Mendoza, for example, were far from savoury.

The way he actually defeated Mendoza was to grab him by the hair and repeatedly punch him about the head until Mendoza subsided to the floor. The fight lasted only 10 minutes. Nor did Mendoza receive any great amount of sympathy for the manner of his defeat. It being felt that he had paid the price of his vanity in allowing his hair to grow long. Most fighters considered it wise to have the hair cropped close to the head or even to be shaved bald to prevent just such an occurrence. Nonetheless none could doubt Mendoza's gameness and, despite losing the title, he was to continue fighting until the age of 57, when he retired and became 'mine host' of the Admiral Nelson pub in his native East End. If anyone was looking for a boxing hero or an instructor then Mendoza would have fitted the bill because he was certainly a fine example of his profession.

It is thought by some authorities that Mendoza created a new style of boxing but this belief is unlikely to stand up to close scrutiny. It is more likely that he modified existing methods in order to overcome the disadvantage of his small stature. In fact there is a story about Mendoza that is worth repeating here because it gives an interesting insight into his personality. It concerns Mendoza's first professional fight, although he won the fight he was not at all pleased with the painful and laboured manner in which he achieved his victory. He reasoned that there was something amiss with his fighting style and promptly retired from the ring for three years in order to improve his skills. It was obviously three years well spent because history has been presented with the fruits of his labour.

This then has been an all too brief account of some of the men and events crucial to the art of bare-fist fighting. Men who both preserved the knowledge of the ancients and added to it some skills of their own. Sadly, it has not been possible to tell of all the brave and skilful men who made important contributions to the art in question. Yet their dedication and efforts were a significant part of the whole scenario of bare-fist fighting. In any case it has to be said that this is a good point at which to depart this particular topic because from this date onwards the art and its practitioners began to move further and further away from the all-in unarmed combat style of fighting and closer to modern day Western boxing which, while effective in its own right, bears little resemblance to its English ancestor.

So far mention has only been made of the men of the 'ring' but it is worth noting that then, as now, there was a female interest and presence in the martial arts. Women who fought with fists and weapons and were just as tough as their male counterparts. Like the men they posted 'Bills of Challenge' which was the traditional way of informing the public of any forthcoming fight. The following is a good example of such a bill.:

I, Elizabeth Wilkinson of Clerkenwell having had some words with Hannah Hyfield and requiring satisfaction do invite her to meet me upon the stage and box me for three guineas; each woman holding half a crown in each hand and the first woman that drops the money to lose the battle.

This forthright challenge was met with an equally forthright answer from the lady in question:

I, Hannah Hyfield of Newgate Market, hearing of the resoluteness of Elizabeth Wilkinson will not fail, God willing, to give her more blows than words, desiring home blows and from her, no favour. She may expect a good thumping!

It should be pointed out, lest the reader suspect that the coins were a device to weight the fist that their use was intended as a means of preventing excessive punishment. In that a contender would tend to drop the coins upon receipt of a heavy blow or the onset of fatigue. In either case the fighter in question would be unable to defend herself and so the dropped coin would automatically stop the fight and therefore the punishment.

Note: While every effort has been made to present accurate facts and figures it has to be pointed out that in the early days of prize-fighting documentation was very sparse. Nor was there any ruling body to organise or regulate the sport. This resulted in a certain amount of confusion, for example, two dates are given for Figg's death (1734 and 1740). In like vein there are other uncertainties such as the actual dates that fighters won or assumed the English title, as in the case of Mendoza (1791 or 1794). In view of this uncertainty the facts presented are those which are most commonly accepted as being accurate.

TECHNICAL FOREWORD

The author makes no claim that the martial techniques in the next section of this book are Anglo-Saxon (early English). Indeed, the techniques illustrated are derived from English sources from the fifteenth century (late middle English) onwards. It is impossible, with any degree of accuracy, for anyone to specify the exact nature or contents (methods and techniques) of early English martial arts. What can safely be said is that numerous Anglo-Saxon manuscript illustrations intimate a link, via the middle English, with those of the modern (mainly pre-renaissance) English.

Experienced martial artists will appreciate the above statement because they understand that there are truisms attending all fighting systems; a martial logic dictating what will (or might) work and what won't. In Oriental martial arts this sees forms and katas, be they unarmed or weaponed, surviving unchanged for centuries because they contain techniques that, all things being equal, work. The same logic may therefore reasonably be employed to suggest that swordsmen and billmen, for example, of sixteenth century England would, essentially, be using similar if not identical methods, to those of their pre-conquest ancestors. Indeed, an English kata (fixed play) dating from at least as early as the 1400's contains methods identical to those in use centuries later.

Double-Armed Fighting

The double-armed, e.g., sword and buckler/sword and dagger techniques illustrated in this book demonstrate initial stances showing the buckler or dagger being held rearwards of the sword (the primary weapon). This contradicts the advice of some contemporary writers who recommended that the secondary weapon be held forward of the sword. The author, after extensive experiment, in the form of full-contact fighting, found that this latter method has inherent weaknesses. For example, the buckler, however small, in certain positions and angles obstructs the vision of its user when held forward of the sword. The dagger, when held forward, does not obstruct the vision but it does offer an uncertain defence against an opposing sword in that it is forever wide-spaced, and would result in false times. Of course, as Silver points out, if your opponent leads with dagger or buckler then you may safely do the same. Although it would seem an act of folly to throw away the advantage given by leading with the sword against an opponent leading with the dagger or buckler. Of course, in an actual engagement there may be times when you choose to advance (pass) the rear foot and use the secondary weapon first. There will also be times, when gathering forward or falling away, when the secondary weapon will momentarily come to the fore but this should be reversed as soon as it is safe to do so. We are of course here talking of single-combat, since on the battlefield it was often necessary, usual in fact, for the leading rank of defensive forces to lead with the shield in order to withstand an enemy's charges (e.g. the Anglo-Saxon shield wall).

Hand Positions

The question arises, when fighting single (with one weapon), of where do you place or keep the empty hand? It is a matter to which the author has applied considerable time, thought, and practise. Rapier and smallsword masters ultimately seem to have advocated, or at least initiated, one of two methods: The first was that of holding the empty hand by the corresponding eye/temple ready to parry a thrust with the palm of the hand (workable as long as you were facing another thrusting weapon): The second was the practise of extending the unused arm behind the body, one supposes as a counterweight to aid balance, especially when lunging. Such methods were really only practicable when fighting (duelling!) against a similarly armed opponent. Eventually such methods became codified into rules of engagement and etiquette, with little consideration being given to battlefield effectiveness. Indeed, artistic merit came to play an increasingly important role in the art of rapier, and particularly of smallsword fighting. Such 'developments' are always likely, or at least possible when the life and death reality of warfare is removed from consideration. Indeed, there is a parallel development in modern Oriental martial arts where the artistic merits of movements assume an importance that almost certainly didn't exist in former, more uncertain, times. The ultimate expression of this approach must surely be Wu Shu (modern) where martial arts have been converted into a synthesized gymnastic dance the purpose of which is to win competitions with artistic interpretations of martial movements.

Stage-gladiators on the other hand used a method whereby, when fighting in the hanging guard (true gardant) the empty hand was held in front of the groin/ lower stomach. The stage-gladiators, although effectively sportsmen, used methods derived from actual warfare. It is possible therefore to discern a link, however far removed, with the said hand position and that probably used by the single-armed warrior. That is to say that the empty hand was likely to be held in front of the body but utilizing the protection of the sword.

Holding the hand as low as did the stage-gladiators is somewhat awkward in terms of balance and coordination not to mention that it contravenes the principle of true space. However, bearing in mind that the people using it were fighting to a set of agreed conventions we can reasonably presume that the disadvantages were equal to both. In other words there was not, effectively, any disadvantage to using it.

However, it is to be considered that on the battlefield there were no rules of conduct, survival was the name of the game. This meant that kicking, punching, gouging, gripping of weapons or weapon hands/arms were all at times necessary. With this in mind the author has felt it necessary to explore all possible alternatives, including those mentioned above. Practical experience has led to a firm conviction that the position demonstrated in this book's illustrations, as regards sword single, is the most effective. This position (a variation of that of the stage-gladiator's) has been found to be the best in terms of combat requirements. That is to say it best allows the fighter, when expedient, to employ such things as punches and grips. The author is therefore reasonably confident that warriors of the past would have used that position, or something very similar, rather than the sporting, or, God forbid, cosmetic and/or artistic poses utilized by some devotees in the past.

8 THE PRINCIPLES OF TRUE FIGHTING

The teachers of traditional English martial arts held that there were certain vital principles which must be adhered to in self-defence. These principles embraced the entire spectrum of the art. They applied not just to the sword, but to battle-axe, quarterstaff, bare-fists, indeed any weapon which a human may use in hand-to-hand combat. The most important of these were known as the 'Four True Times', 'Four False Times', the 'Four Grounds' and the 'Four Governors'. The observation of these principles is vital if you are to practise English martial arts with any degree of safety and effectiveness. They must be studied and thoroughly understood before any attempt is made at mastering the techniques. Even if you practise another style of martial art you are strongly recommended to utilize the tenets contained in this chapter.

The Four True Times

1. the time of the hand.
2. the time of the hand and body.
3. the time of the hand, body and foot.
4. the time of the hand, body and feet.

The Four False Times

1. the time of the foot.
2. the time of the foot and body.
3. the time of the foot, body and hand.
4. the time of the feet, body and hand.

The idea behind these two sets of times is simple, it is a method of telling you the fastest and safest and the slowest and riskiest order of moving in a fight. Let us go through them one by one.

The True Times refer, in descending order, to the comparative speeds of movement of various parts of the body. The time of the hand is fastest of all. In

93

other words it can move faster than any other part of the body. Then comes the time of the hand and body, slower than the hand alone but faster than moving hand, body and foot. This latter time is in turn faster than moving hand, body and both feet.

The False Times, these present the opposite truth, that of the comparative slowness of various parts of the body. For example moving the foot and body is slower than moving the foot alone, which in turn is slower than moving just the hand. Moving hand, body, and both feet is slower than moving the hand, body, and one foot. If you compare true times against false times you will see that the 'fastest' false time, that of moving the foot is slower than the fastest of the true times, that of moving the hand. The first four times are called the True Times because they give the safest order of movement in a fight. It should be pointed out that these rules largely apply during actual attacks and defences, because there can be situations were two opponents may just be circling each other prior to any engagement, in which case the hand may well be static whilst the feet are of course moving.

The second four times are called the False Times because they will create openings which your opponent may take advantage of. It can do no harm to give an example of how these principles work. Supposing that two swordsmen are facing each other but out of range. One moves his hand, (i.e. positions his sword) and then steps forward, he has used a True Time. His opponent however steps forward first and then positions his sword, he has used a False Time. This means that the user of the true time is now free to attack the false time user whose sword would not be in place to prevent the attack. Of course, as all martial artists know, circumstances often dictate that you are, in a fight, sometimes unable to do the things that you want to do. However, as in all things, if we do not practise along the right lines we have no chance of achieving them in a real situation.

The Four Grounds

1. Judgement
2. Distance
3. Time
4. Place

In the case of **the Four Grounds,** Judgement means the ability to maintain the optimum distance between yourself and your adversary. The optimum Distance is to be out of striking range of your opponent but close enough to take advantage of any openings that occur. Time is that moment when you may safely attack your opponent without him being able to immediately reciprocate. Place refers to an opening in his defence through which you may deliver your attack. Through Judgement you keep your Distance, through Distance you get your Time, through Time you safely win the Place in which to strike your opponent.

The Four Governors

1. Judgement
2. Measure
3. Pressing In
4. Flying Out

In the case of **the Four Governors**, Judgement is to know when you can safely attack your opponent, or when he may do the same to you. Measure is to keep your space true, that is to say to maintain an effective guard and to be able to recognise when your opponent's guard leaves you an opening through which to attack him. In other words it means positioning yourself and your weapon in such a way that you are able to strike your opponent while denying him the same opportunity. Pressing In, is attacking, which must only be done after you have 'won the place' which is to say that you should only attack after you have created a safe opening in the opponent's defence. Flying Out, means to disengage from your attack, or that of your opponent. The term itself (Flying Out) obviously indicates that the disengagement must be carried out speedily. It is a matter of some importance to always regard the third and fourth governors with one mind, not to think of the third without instantaneously according some thought to the fourth.

Keep these principles in mind at all times and remember that the techniques that will be revealed in this book are entirely dependent upon the above for successful application.

Common sense tells us that the Company of Maisters would have been required to teach the 'True Fight' according to an approved or acceptable syllabus. In keeping with this approach every care has been taken to ensure, as far as is humanly possible, that the techniques, principles and philosophies contained in this modest treatise have been taken from the 'True Fight' as taught by authentic maisters of defence.

The prime concern of this section is to discuss and explain the stances contained in the system. Any martial artist will understand what is meant by the term stance. Equally they will appreciate the importance of accurate and effective stance work.

In English martial arts there were a plethora of names and terms which, generally speaking, referred to stances. Our forebears would have been quite familiar with the following terms: ward, guard, posture, lying, fight, attitude, all of which were ways of describing a stance. The given terms were more or less interchangeable. However, it is the author's intention to provide certain of these terms with specific meanings so as to more conveniently explain the art. This approach will in no way contradict the teachings of the maisters.

From this point onwards the term guard will refer to the actual position in which the weapon is being held. That is to say the position in which the weapon is placed to await an attack. For example if the weapon is held so as to cover the right side of the body it will be deemed an outside guard. If it is held so as to protect the left side of the body it will be termed an inside guard. The expression ward will be used to refer to an actual movement of the weapon. Let us give an example of this; the defender (the patient agent) is standing with his weapon held on an inside guard. His attacker (the agent) aims a blow at the patient agent's right shoulder. The patient agent is now forced to move his weapon across to his right side to defend against that blow. In other words the patient has warded to the outside from an inside guard.

The reasons for these distinctions may seem self-evident but that was not always so. For the technical jargon of the maisters varied according to the custom and language of their generation. In like vein we have to consider the actual manner of holding the weapon, because here again confusion can easily arise. As a rule the maisters used the terms guard, ward, etc. not only to denote the area of the body being defended (or attacked) but also to describe the manner in which the weapon was being held. Unfortunately, apart from being a somewhat clumsy method of definition, it also suffers the misfortune of inadequacy. Let us take for an example the outside guard. This guard can be made with the tip of the weapon pointing upwards or downwards. In like manner it can be made with the weapon held high or low. In fact there are various differences which the terms guard, ward, etc. do not always indicate. Solving this latter problem has been made somewhat easier by Silver who gave names to some of these positions: close fight, and gardant fight, being two examples of his definitions. The meaning of these 'fights' will be given a little later. So, to recap, there is the guard, meaning the position in which the weapon awaits the attack. Then comes the ward, meaning the act of moving to meet the attack. And, finally comes the fight, meaning the manner in which the weapon is held and used.

The evolution of weapons and warfare created various schools of thought within ancient martial arts. This applied in England as much as any other country. Consequently different 'styles' abounded. However by sticking to the principles of the true fight it will be found that there are five guards which form the basis of

English martial arts. It should be pointed out that these guards themselves do have variants, as in the case, for example, of: true gardant, and bastard gardant.

Basic Stances

Before the actual fighting techniques of English martial arts can be discussed it will be necessary to consider the stances and footwork which form their foundation. English martial arts, like any authentic fighting system, are based upon proven principles and philosophies. Without a sound knowledge of these a person's martial technique will be flawed. Or, to use an ancient English expression that person will be fighting a 'false fight'. Therefore please take the time to both read and put into practise the following information.

The Outside Guard

As its name implies is the position held by the weapon to protect the outside or right side of the body. In practise this means anything to the right of the user's weapon. The outside guard, also known as the dexter guard, is shown in Figure 5 (overleaf).

The Inside Guard

A mirror image of the outside guard, the inside guard protects the left side of the body. That is to say anything on the inside or left of the weapon. This guard is also known as the sinister guard (see Figure 6).

The Medium Guard

Figure 7 shows the medium guard. It is immediately apparent that this guard falls between the inside and the outside guard. Over the centuries this guard has been both praised and damned. There were those who said it should never be used because it was an 'uncertain defence'. And there were those who regarded it as the finest defence of all. Indeed there were maisters who believed that the medium to be the only true guard, and that all other guards were merely transitory positions to which the swordsman warded when fighting, their idea being that the medium is the guard in which all moves start and finish. The medium guard is also known as the unicorn guard.

The St George Guard

Tradition has it that this is the guard used by St George whilst slaying the infamous dragon. Also known as the diameter guard it has one office and one office only, to defend against a vertically descending cut or blow at the head. A powerful defence against the said blow but a potentially risky one in that it leaves the rest of the body exposed to attack from a different angle (see Figure 8).

The Hanging Guard

Also known as the pendant guard, this was the true gardant fight referred to by the maisters of defence. As with the medium guard it was the subject of much contention between the maisters. There were those who despised the guard, and those who said, " ... the Pendant or hanging guard is the surest and best guard that can be made... ". Strangely enough even those who disliked this guard were forced to admit that it was the best guard to use when being sorely pressed or attacked by more than one person. It seems that it was seen by many as a 'retreating' guard which might explain the antipathy which it incurred. It seems probable that a guard which was so strong defensively would provide a sound foundation for the brave man to press forward. Indeed such was the case with one m[r]. Johnson, a famous stage-gladiator, who fought his bouts mainly from the hanging guard. And whereas most fighters used this guard when 'gathered upon', it was said of m[r] Johnson that he; " ...advances with it, and maintains it through the whole battle with unshaken firmness". Figure 9 shows the hanging guard/ true gardant.

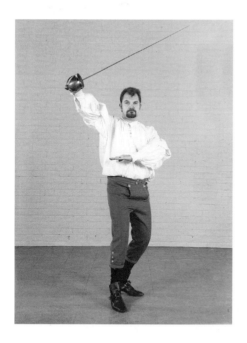

Figure 5 Outside Guard

Figure 6 Inside Guard

Figure 7 Medium Guard

Figure 8 St George Guard

Figure 9 Hanging Guard/True Gardant

As hinted at earlier, there was in existence a method of cataloguing the different methods of holding and using the broadsword. This system divided the methods into four groups, and whilst no claims can be made that this is an all encompassing system of classification it yet remains a useful method of subdividing the art of the sword.

1. Gardant Fight
2. Open Fight
3. Close Fight
4. Variable Fight

1. Gardant Fight

To fight gardant is to fight using the hanging guard. In fact the very name Gardant Fight indicates the amazing continuity of English broadsword fighting, because when the stage-gladiators referred to the hanging guard as the best defensive stance of all they were echoing the knowledge of the earlier maisters of defence who named this stance after its purpose, e.g., guarding. Gardant fight is divided into two types, that of true gardant and that of bastard gardant. Both true and bastard gardant mean that the sword is held with the hilt uppermost and the tip pointing towards the ground. In the case of true gardant the hilt is held above the head, whereas with the bastard gardant the hilt is held at chest height, or lower.

2. Open Fight

This is to hold the hand and hilt above the head with the blade vertical or sloping somewhat to the rear. This guard probably found most currency in tightly packed groups on the battlefield. This fight should only be used when fighting double. That is to say when you have a shield or additional weapon in the left hand.

3. Close Fight

This name is descriptive of its function, it means to fight at the half-sword, that is to say with the swords close enough to cross at the mid-point of their blades. This would apply whether the sword was pointing up or down. As a general rule, combatants avoided blade contact unless defending or knocking the opponent's blade aside.

4. Variable Fight

This is a general purpose name used to describe any method of fighting which does not fit into the three categories given above. It would for example cover the fighting methods of an unskilled fighter but it seems chiefly to have been used to define methods originating from foreign climes.

Additional Fighting Terms

There are certain other terms which will be encountered in these pages so it will be as well to account for them now.

Chopping: To 'chop' is to deliver a blow in line with the weapon's position with no twist of the wrist.

Darting: This is to slip or withdraw the weapon away from the opponent and suddenly to thrust back again in the same line.

Falling Away: To fall away is to reverse the above by moving the rear foot backwards and bringing the front foot back to it (maintaining the relative distance between the feet).

False Fight: To fight without knowledge or use of the principles of the art.

Falsing or falsifying: This is to fake an attack in order to tempt the opponent's weapon out of position and so 'win the place' (create an opening).

Flirting: To flirt is to withdraw the weapon somewhat and then immediately return it to its original position. It is intended to confuse your opponent and keep him unsettled, but it was frowned on by some as being a risky manoeuvre because withdrawing the weapon weakens the defensive posture.

Footwork: Swordplay is subject to exactly the same principles and footwork as bare-fist fighting. At all times remember that simplicity is efficiency's best friend. To keep this in mind ponder the sentiments of one sixteenth century English maister of defence when considering foreign methods of swordplay:

> …because they in their Rapier-Fight stand upon so manie intricate trickes, that in all the course of a mans life it shall be hard to learn them, and if they misse in doing the least of them in their fight they are in danger of death.

Full Force: refers to a state when a blow has achieved optimum speed and power. To meet a blow before it is in full force is to block (stop) the weapon or arm before that optimum state has been achieved.

Gathering Forward: To gather forward is to advance the leading foot and bring the rear foot up to it (maintaining relative distance between the feet).

Inclosing: Also known as enclosing, or commanding, this is the act of stepping up to your opponent and seizing the weapon or the weapon arm. It is only attempted after the opponent's attack has been nullified.

Lurching: To lurch is to deliberately leave an opening in your defence in order to tempt your opponent into making an attack that you are ready to take advantage of.

Narrow Spaced: This term indicates that your weapon is holding the correct line thereby leaving no gap through which you may be attacked.

The Pass: This is the same movement known as the throw in bare-fist fighting. It properly refers to a full step which advances the rear foot to the front.

The Place: This is taken to mean the most effective position of the weapon for defence and attack. To win the place is to force or trick the opponent's weapon out of line to allow an attack. To lose the place is to allow your adversary to do the same thing.

Sliding: To slide is to slide your weapon along that of your opponent and then to suddenly disengage and attack in a different line.

The Slip: This usually refers to pulling the weapon away from an attack but the term was also used to describe the act of moving the leading leg away from a blow aimed specifically at that limb. In this latter event the withdrawal of the leg was usually combined with a simultaneous blow at the opponent's head.

The Square: The feet are held at ninety degrees to each other, or as close to this angle as efficiency and comfort permit. The actual distance between the feet will be dependent upon the stature of the individual.

Throwing: To 'throw' the weapon is to deliver a cut with a powerful twisting action of the wrist.

Time: Is that specific moment during which you may attack your adversary without risk to yourself. Time is heavily dependent upon measure and space.

The Traverse: To step to one side of your opponent, it also can mean actually circling around your opponent to keep him off-balance and at the same time to seek an opening to attack him.

True Fight: To fight according to the principles of the art.

Variations: A certain amount of latitude is permissible as long as the variation is not sufficient to adversely affect balance, strength, etc. The only stance out of the five which does not always use the square is the St George's stance because it sometimes demands that you withdraw the leading leg parallel to the trailing leg. There are two reasons for this action. Firstly so that the strength from both legs is directly under the weapon and, secondly, since the leading leg loses the protection of the weapon, it must be withdrawn to comparative safety, usually when defending against pole-arms. Against swords it is possible to use the St George with a square stance.

The Vault: To pivot on one foot and swing the other foot around in a semi-circular movement to move the body from one line to another, either to avoid an attack or gain an advantageous position.

Wheeling: To 'wheel' the weapon is to swing it in a complete circle with the hand above the head and pass it behind the back in order to bring it to an attacking position in front of the body. It should only be used as a follow up to a 'false', a block, or an actual attack, though it may also be used after stepping away from an attack, as for example after vaulting. It is a method which adds great power to a block or strike but must be used with the utmost caution since it momentarily leaves the body completely unguarded.

Whirling: Whirling is the act of spinning or twirling your weapon in fast, powerful 360 degree revolutions using the wrist as the pivot point.

Wide Spaced: This means that your weapon is so far from its correct defensive position that an opening is created through which your opponent may attack.

Wrenching: Wrenching is a single 360 degree spin of the weapon, it is a means of attacking in a different line to the one you were previously engaged in. For example if you are engaged at the half-sword in a forehand ward you could spin the sword underneath your opponent's weapon and attack underneath his blade.

These then are the basic movements that you will be required to learn and understand. Once you are comfortable with them you can move on to the techniques.

Figure 10 Basket-hilted sword from the wreck of the Mary Rose,
an English warship which sank in 1545
Photo: the Mary Rose Trust

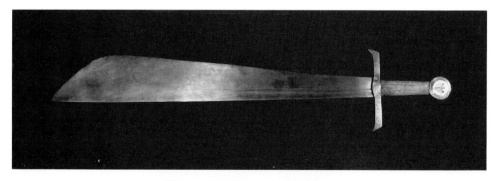

Figure 11 Conyer's falchion
Photo: the Dean and Chapter of Durham Cathedral

BROADSWORD

Technique 1

a. Agent and patient agent face each other in true gardant.

b. Agent (left) wrenches vertically descending cut to the patient agent's head.

c. Patient agent gathers forward and stops (blocks) the blow before it is in full force using the true gardant, he simultaneously blocks the agent's sword wrist with his left hand.

d. In a continuous action the patient agent pushes the agent's sword arm outwards and downwards while simultaneously wrenching a blow to his head.

Technique 2

a. Agent and patient agent face each other in the inside guard

b. Agent (left) throws a cut to patient agent's right neck

c. Patient agent meets the attack by warding to an outside guard.

d. The patient agent passes with his left foot, simultaneously pushing the agent's sword arm across his (the agent's) body. The patient agent completes the move by wrenching a cut to the agent's leading leg.

Technique 3

a. Agent and patient agent face each other in the outside guard.

b. Agent (right) throws a cut to patient agent's left neck. The patient agent
   defends by warding to an inside guard.

c. The patient agent gathers forward and wrenches an outside blow to the agent's leading leg. At the same time he uses his left hand to push the agent's sword hand out of line.

Technique 4

a. The patient agent stands in the outside guard, and the agent faces him in the true gardant.

b. The agent (right) wrenches an overhead blow to the patient agent's head. The patient agent stops the blow by warding to the St George guard.

c. The patient agent vaults to his right and wheels an inside cut to the agent's body while at the same time blocking the agent's sword hand.

a. Agent and patient agent face each other in the true gardant.

b. Agent (right) wrenches an inside cut at the patient agent's leading leg. the patient agent stops the blow by warding to a bastard gardant.

c. The patient agent now vaults to his right and wrenches a blow to the agent's wrist.

Technique 6

a. Agent and patient agent are both in the true gardant.

b. Agent (left) wrenches an overhead blow at patient agent's head.

c. The patient agent meets the blow with a St George before it is in full force.

d. The patient agent now vaults out of line and simultaneously throws a blow at the agent's wrist.

Technique 7

a. Both men are in an outside guard.

b. The Agent (right) throws an inside cut at the patient agent's sword wrist.

c. The patient agent slips the blow by raising his sword arm. The force of the agent's blow, having met no resistance, pulls him off-balance.

d. The patient agent now chops down at the agent's sword arm.

Technique 8

a. Both men adopt an outside guard.

b. The agent throws a blow to his opponent's head. The patient agent stops this with a St George guard.

c. The patient agent now vaults to his right and throws a blow at the agent's wrist.

Technique 9

a. Agent and patient agent are both in an inside guard.

b. Agent throws a cut to the right neck of his opponent. The patient agent
stops the attack by warding to an outside guard.

c. The agent now wrenches an inside cut to the patient agent's leading leg.

d. The patient agent stops the second attack with a low inside guard.

e. The patient agent completes the move by turning up the point of his sword and thrusting to the agent's body.

Technique 10

a. Agent and patient agent are both in true gardant.

b. Agent (right) wrenches an overhead blow to patient agent's head. The defender stops the blow with a St George guard.

c. The agent responds by wrenching a blow to the outside of the patient agent's leading leg.

d. Patient agent stops the secondary attack by warding to a bastard gardant.

e. The patient agent passes with his left foot, at the same time using his left hand to push the agent's sword arm away. He completes the move with a slashing cut to the agent's body.

BROADSWORD
GRIPS

Technique 1

a. Both men are in an inside guard.

b. The agent (left) aims a blow at the patient agent's right neck. The patient
agent stops the attack by warding to an outside guard.

126

c. The patient agent passes with his left foot and grips the agent's sword wrist.

d. The patient agent now twists the agent's arm to off-balance him and delivers a blow to his left neck.

127

Technique 2

a. Both men are in an inside guard.

b. The agent (right) steps forward and delivers an outside cut at the patient agent's right side. The patient agent stops this by warding to an outside

c. The patient agent reaches forward and catches the agent's sword wrist.

d. The patient agent passes with his left foot, pulls the agent's sword arm to his rear and simultaneously smashes his sword hilt into the agent's jaw.

e. The patient agent completes the move with a drawing cut to the agent's neck.

Technique 3

a. Agent and patient agent are both in an outside guard.

b. The agent (left) aims an inside cut at his opponent's left neck. The patient agent gathers forward and stops the blow by warding to true gardant.

c. The agent passes with his left foot and grips the patient agent's sword wrist.

d. The patient agent responds by gripping the agent's left wrist from the outside, he then immediately pivots to his left.

e. The patient agent twists the agent's arm and simultaneously pulls him downwards. From here he is free to deliver any attack he should choose.

a. Agent and patient agent face each other in true gardant.

b. The agent (right) steps forward and wrenches an inside cut at his opponent.
The patient agent gathers forward and stops the blow with true gardant.

c. The patient agent passes with his left foot, reaches underneath his own sword arm and wraps his left arm around the agent's sword arm (from the outside) and exerts pressure against the elbow.

d. The patient agent vaults and pivots to his right so as to exert more pressure to the agent's arm and at the same time move away from any potential counter-attack. From here he can either demand a surrender or deliver a blow.

a. Agent and patient agent adopt an outside guard.

b. The agent (left) aims an inside cut at his opponent. The defender stops the attack with an inside guard.

c. The patient agent reaches forward and grips the agent's sword wrist from the outside.

d. The patient agent pulls the agent towards him, twisting the agent's arm, and simultaneously smashes his sword hilt into the agent's face.

e. The patient agent kicks the agent's leading leg from under him.

f. The patient agent threatens the fallen man.

QUARTERSTAFF

Technique 1

a. Both men are in the medium guard.

b. Agent (left) gathers forward and aims a blow at patient agent's left temple. The
defender stops the attack with an inside guard.

c. The patient agent, having pushed the agent's staff wide, wrenches a blow around
the outside of the agent's staff to attack his right knee.

Technique 2

a. Both men adopt the medium guard.

141

b. Agent (right) aims an inside blow to the patient agent's head. The patient agent stops this by warding to an outside guard.

c. The patient agent continues the move to force the agent's staff to the ground.

d. The patient agent whips his staff up to deliver an inside blow to the agent's head.

Technique 3

a. Agent and patient agent are both in the medium guard.

b. The agent (left) gathers forward and thrusts at his opponent's stomach. The patient agent puts aside the thrust by warding to the hanging guard.

c. The patient agent now raises the tip of his staff and delivers a thrust to the agent's body.

144

a. Both men are in a medium guard.

b. The agent (left) thrusts to the patient agent's body. The patient agent puts the
   attack aside by warding to a hanging guard.

c. The patient agent begins to wrench an overhead blow by pulling the tip of his staff down past his own legs and bringing it over his head.

d. The patient agent completes the move by landing the blow on the agent's head.

a. Agent and patient agent are in the medium guard.

b. The agent (left) gathers forward and thrusts at the patient agent's foremost hand. The patient agent flies back and simultaneously raises his staff.

147

c. The patient agent counter attacks with a blow to the agent's head.

Technique 6

a. Agent and patient agent are in the medium guard.

b. The agent (left) throws a blow to the inside of the patient agent's lower leg.

c. The patient agent slips the attack to his leg and simultaneously raises his staff.

d. The patient agent completes the move with a strike to the agent's head.

Technique 7

a. Agent and patient agent are in the medium guard.

b. The agent (left) gathers forward and aims a blow at his his opponent's head.

c. The patient agent stops the attack by slipping his hands to a halfstaff grip and assuming the St George guard.

151

d. The agent completes the move by pivoting to his left and striking at the agent's left temple, slipping back to a quarterstaff grip as he does so.

Technique 8

a. The agent and patient agent are in a medium guard.

b. The agent (right) aims a blow at his opponents head. The patient agent stops the blow by warding to a St George guard.

c. The patient agent passes with his left foot and forces the agent's staff backwards by firmly sliding his own staff down the agent's staff – towards the agent's hands.

d. The patient agent completes the move by kicking the agent in the *coddes* (testicles).

Technique 9

a. Both men are in a medium guard.

b. The agent (right) aims an inside blow at the patient agent's left temple. The patient agent stops this by warding to an inside guard.

c. The patient agent lets go of his own staff with his left hand and grips the agent's staff.

d. The patient agent begins to raise his staff and simultaneously twists the agent's staff outwards.

e. Continuing the twisting action the patient agent drives the butt (bottom) of his staff into the agent's chest.

a. Both men are in a medium guard.

b. The agent (right) steps forward and thrusts at the patient agent's face. The patient agent *puts aside* the thrust by warding to an inside guard.

157

c. The patient agent now forces the attacker's staff to the ground.

d. The agent, realizing his danger, attempts to *fly back*. The patient agent, to cover the extra distance, *thrusts single* at the agent's body.

SWORD & DAGGER

Technique 1

a. The fighters face each other in an outside guard

b. The agent (left) throws an inside blow at his opponent. The patient agent stops the attack by warding to the true gardant.

c. The agent passes with his left foot and thrusts to the patient agent's body with his dagger. The patient agent 'puts aside' the agents dagger by turning down the point of his own dagger and warding to his left.

d. The patient agent uses his dagger to control the agent's sword and wrenches an inside cut to his left neck, taking care to lean away from his dagger.

161

Technique 2

a. Agent and patient agent are both in outside guards.

b. The agent (right) throws an oblique blow at the patient agent's head. The defender stops the blow with his dagger.

c. The agent wrenches a secondary attack to the outside of the patient agent's thigh. The defender stops the attack by warding to a low outside.

d. The patient agent passes and cuts the agent's sword arm with his dagger.

e. The patient agent ends the move with a sword slash to the agent's stomach.

Technique 3

a. Agent and patient agent are both in outside guards.

b. The agent (left) thrusts at the patient agent's body. The patient agent moves to his right and simultaneously 'puts aside' the thrust with his dagger.

c. The patient agent chops down at his opponent's head with his sword. The agent stops the blow with his dagger.

d. The patient agent wrenches a blow around the outside of his opponent's dagger to land a blow on the inside of his leading leg.

Sword & Dagger
vs
Sword & Buckler

Technique 1

a. Both fighters lead with their swords held in outside guards.

b. The agent (left) steps forward and throws an inside cut at his opponent's left neck. The patient agent stops the attack with his buckler.

c. In a continuous action the patient agent knocks the agent's sword away.
(It was normal to deflect blows with bucklers rather than meet them head
on).

d. The patient agent vaults to his left (away from danger) and simultaneously
chops down at the agent's sword arm.

Technique 2

a. Both men lead with their swords in outside guards.

b. The agent (left) attempts to throw an inside cut at the agent's neck. The patient agent stops the attack with his buckler.

c. The agent wrenches a blow to the outside of his opponent's right leg. The patient agent responds by warding to a low outside guard.

d. The patient agent turns up his sword and thrusts the agent in the stomach.

e. Should the agent manage to put aside or evade the thrust the patient agent
can follow up by passing and driving his buckler into the agent's face.

Technique 3

a. Both men lead with swords held in outside guards.

b. The agent (left) attempts to throw a blow at the patient agent's left side. The patient agent meets the blow before it is in full force and starts to deflect it.

c. Having deflected the agent's sword out and down the defender chops down onto his attacker's dagger wrist.

173

d. Immediately following his sword blow the patient agent whips the rim of
   his buckler into the agent's neck.

THE BILL

Technique 1

a. Both men have adopted the medium guard.

b. The agent (left) gathers forward and thrusts at his opponent. The patient agent responds by using the blade of his bill to *put aside* the thrust and make his opponent *wide spaced*.

c. The patient agent gathers forward, simultaneously raising his weapon, and chops down at the agent's head. The agent responds by slipping his hands to a halfstaff grip and warding to a St George guard.

d. Using the blade, the patient agent hooks the agent's staff downwards.

e. The patient agent now thrusts to his opponent's body.

Technique 2

a. The fighters are in medium guard.

b. The agent (left) thrusts at the patient agent.

c. The patient agent responds by rotating the bill and blocking the agent's weapon
   downwards with the flat of the blade, keeping the prongs either side of the pole.

d. He continues pressing until he has forced the head of the agent's bill to the ground. Note that the prongs of the patient agent's bill have trapped the shaft of the agent's weapon.

e. The patient agent, using the groove formed by the prongs of his blade, runs his bill up the staff of the agent's bill to attack his hand.

f. The patient agent gathers forward and thrusts at the agent's throat in such a manner that the prongs go either side of it.

a. The sword and buckler man is in an outside guard. The billman is in a medium guard.

b. The agent (left) advances to his right.

c. The agent passes and uses his buckler to put aside the bill.

d. The agent aims a blow at the billman's foremost hand.

e. The billman traverses to his left, simultaneously changing his grip by slipping the shaft of his bill through his left hand.

f. The billman passes and wrenches an overhead blow at the agent's sword arm with the butt of the bill. Note that he slides the shaft back through the left hand to increase range and power.

g. The billman passes with his right foot and wrenches an overhead blow at the agent's head, once again slipping his hands to add range and power.

Technique 4

a. The sword and buckler man is in an outside guard. The billman is in a *reverse gardant.*

b. The agent (left) raises his buckler to prevent the overhead blow and steps forward to deliver a thrust.

c. The billman steps back on his left foot and brings the flat of his blade down to block the thrust.

d. After making contact, the billman forces the agent's sword to the ground.

e. Keeping the blade flat the billman whips it up and thrusts at the agent's chest or
   throat.

BARE-FIST FIGHTING

a. The agent (right) grabs patient agent and threatens him.

Technique 1

b. The patient agent grips agent's right wrist and twists outwards and at the same time pushes his left shoulder backwards.

c. The patient agent kicks agent's right leg from under him.

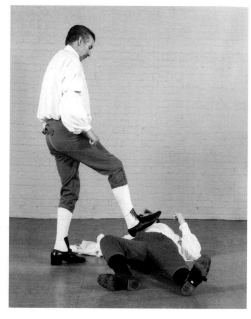

d. The patient agent completes the move with a stamp to the body.

a. The agent (left) throws a right jab at the patient agent's face. The patient agent stops it with a left forearm guard.

b. The patient agent moves his body weight forward and delivers a straight right to the agent's face.

c. The agent (left) aims a punch at the patient agent's face. The patient agent stops it with a forearm block.

Technique 3

a. The patient agent grabs the agent's right arm with his left hand, grips him around the body with his right arm and steps behind him.

b. Pivoting to his left, the patient agent leans forward, lifts the agent into the air and throws him to the ground. This is the throw known as the 'cross-buttock'.

a. The agent (left) grabs the patient agent's shirt front to threaten him.

b. The patient agent places his right foot behind the agent's left heel at a right angle to it, he simultaneously grabs his right arm to control it.

Technique 4

c. The patient agent leans forward and presses his knee against the agent's and forces the joint backwards, at the same time pushing him with his right hand.

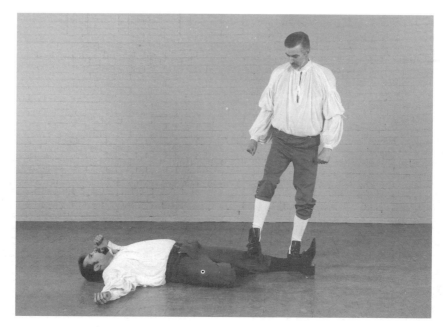

d. Once the agent has hit the ground the patient agent stamps on his knee.

Technique 5

a. The agent (right) grips the patient agent's right wrist.

b. The patient agent responds by gripping the agent's wrist and forcing his arm up against the joint.

c. The patient agent hits up against the elboe joint with his left hand.

d. The patient agent completes the move with a leg-sweep.

Technique 6

a. The agent aims a punch at the patient agent's stomach which he stops with a low forearm guard.

b. The patient agent wrenches a backfist blow to the agent's face.

c. The patient agent completes the move with a straight right to the agent's jaw.

a. The agent (left) throws a hook to land underneath the patient agent's left ear. The patient agent stops this by rotating his left elbow upwards.

b. The patient agent then counters by throwing a backfist into the agent's face.

Technique 8

a. The agent (left) attempts a right hook into his opponent's ribs. The patient agent defends by pulling his elbow to his side.

b. The patient agent drives a straight left at the agent's jaw.

Technique 9

a. The agent (right) aims a left jab at his opponent's solar plexus. The patient agent stops this by dropping his right arm across his stomach.

b. The patient agent counters with a left hammer-fist under the agent's left ear.

Technique 10

a. The agent (right) aims a straight right at his opponent's face. The patient agent stops it and knocks it to the side with a high forearm block.

b. The patient agent completes the move with a kick to the 'coddles'.

Stances

Medium guard

Inside guard

202

Outside guard

Low outside guard

Low inside guard

St George guard – square stance

St George guard – parallel stance

Hanging guard

Reverse gardant

Outside guard

Inside guard

St George guard – square stance

St George guard – parallel stance

True gardant

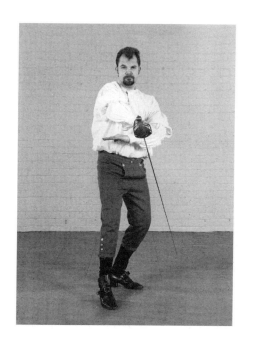

Bastard gardant

Medium guard

Lower outside guard

 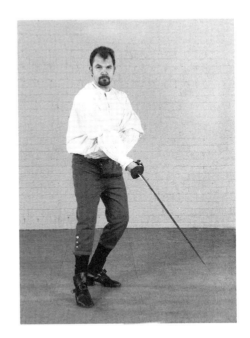

Low inside guard

Medium guard

Inside guard

Outside guard

Low inside guard

Low outside guard

St George guard – square stance

St George guard – parallel stance

Hanging guard

Reverse gardant

Outside guard

Hanging guards

Outside guard

Open fight

Buckler leading

Rapier style

Sword and dagger

S
T
A
N
C
E
S

Basic stance

Upper block

Lower block

Defence against hooks to the head

Defence against hooks to the side

Defence against a stomach punch

WORDS OF WISDOM

Students of Oriental martial arts will be well aware of the importance placed by their masters upon philosophical and moral teaching. The English maisters of defence were no different in this respect. Many of their guidelines were contained in their Company's oaths, letters and constitution but fighting philosophies and general maxims were taught seperately. It is our good fortune that much of this martial and secular advice was included in the published works of those maisters who chose to share their knowledge more widely. This short chapter is devoted to presenting some of those teachings. In certain cases the wording has been altered slightly to assist clarity.

Silver

It is to be considered that man by so much the more waxeth fearfull or boulde by how much the more he knoweth how to avoid or not to enshew danger.

Whosoever mindeth to exercise himselfe in this true and honorable Art or Science, it is requisite that he be indued with deep judgement, a valiant hart and great activitie, in which three qualities this exercise doth as it were delight, live and florish.

Fencing in this new fangled age is like our fashion, every day a change, resembling the chameleon who altereth himself into all colours save white. So fencing changeth into all wards save the right.

There is nothing permanent that is not true, what can be true that is uncertain? How can that be certain that stands upon uncertain grounds?

There is no doubt but that the honourable exercise of the weapon is made right perfect by means of two things, to wit: Judgement and Force: Because by the one we know the manner and time to handle the weapon, and by the other we have the power to execute therewith, in due time with advantage.

Let every man that is desirous to practise this Art endeavour himself to get strength and agility of body, assuring himself that Judgement without this activity and force availeth little or nothing: Yea, happily giveth occasion of hurt and spoil. For men being blinded in their own judgements, and presuming thereon, because they know how and what they ought to do give many times the onset and enterprise yet never perform it in act.

The Noble Science of Defence is to be preferred next to Divinity; for as Divinity preserveth the soul from hell and the devil, so doth the Noble Science defend the body from wounds and slaughter. And moreover the exercising of weapons putteth away aches, griefs, and diseases, it increaseth strength, and sharpens the wits, it giveth a perfect Judgement, it expelleth melancholy, choleric, and evil conceits, it keepeth a man in breath, perfect health, and long life.

None can judge of the craft but the craftsman.

Godfrey

The deficiency of strength may be greatly supplied by Art; but the want of Art will have but heavy succour from strength.

True honour must be very intimate with honesty.

Killing a man, when you are forced upon the defensive, clears you in human laws; but how far you are justified in Christianity the Gospel can best tell you. There is a Consciousness attends all actions, which is the strongest monitor; and that Consciousness will not leave a man undisturbed after his fellow-creature is laid bleeding at his feet, though from the highest provocation, and in his necessary self-defence.

Lonnergan

Labour to parry well, rather than to hit at random by too much ambition or heat of passion.

Let courage and prudence be your inseparable guides in the execution of your attacks, defences, and counter attacks.

Self-opinion is often hurtful, yet none at all is much more so.

Undertake no more than what you are certain of performing.

Stand always on guard first, but out of measure of your enemy.

Seem to fear a forward fencer so that you may gain some advantage over him.

Attack a timid fencer briskly; you will disconcert all his measures and put him in disorder.

Be not over elated by the attacks you succeed with, nor despise those that succeed against you.

Study the danger and advantage of every attack that you make,

McBane

After points are presented, you must take care of yourself for there's no Time given.

Don't trust anyone not to be base and villainous.

To avoid desperate combats my advice is for all gentlemen to take a hearty cup, and to drink friends to avoid trouble.

Brown

Simplicity is efficiency's best friend.

Blackwell

Courage in a Man is a good Property, but Skill with Courage is better.

Egan

PUGILISTS! as your endeavours may stimulate you to improve in your science, be not unmindful to increase in CHARACTER. Lift not your arm against the weak, intemperate, or the ignorant, who might provoke you to ridiculous combat... Keep from boasting as it not only shows weakness of mind, but generally ends in disgrace.

THE COMPANY OF MAISTERS

Mastery of the basic techniques given in this book will enable a student to seek entry to The Company of Maisters as a free scholler. For information about the Company and details of courses and tuition please contact:

Anciant Maister Terry Brown
Frithgarth, Brandon Road
Hockwold-cum-Wilton
Norfolk IP26 4NQ England

BIBLIOGRAPHY

Adams, J. D. 1932 *The Swords of the Vikings*

Anderson, J. 1881 *Ancient Scottish Weapons*

Anglin, J. P. Autumn 1984 *The Schools of Defence in Elizabethan London*

Ascham, R. 1545 *Toxophilus*

Ayscough, W. 1714 *The Inn-Play or Cornish Hugg Wrestler*

Aylward, J. D. 1956 *The English Master of Arms…*

Borer, Cathcart, Mary 1977 *The City of London*

Boulton, W. B. 1901 *The Amusements of Old London*

Branston, Brian 1957 *Lost Gods of England*

Briggs, A. 1983 *A Social History of England*

Broughton, John 1743 *Proposals for erecting an Amphitheatre*

Brown, Rawdon (ed.) 1873 *Calendar of State Papers, Venetian, Vol. 5, 1534-54*

Bryant, A. 1977 *The Age of Chivalry*

Bulstrode, Sir P. 1721 *Memories and Reflections*

Campell, Lord A. 1894 *Notes on Swords from Culloden*

Castle, E. 1884 *Schools and Masters of Defence*

Chambers, R (ed.) 1863 *The Book of Days*

Chambers, E. K. & Greg, W. W. (edited by) *The Remembrancia* (of London)

Chancellor, Valerie, E. 1967 Medieval and Tudor Britain

Crosnier, R. 1965 Fencing with the Sabre

Cunningham, P. 1848 A Life of the Architect

Davidson, H. R. E. 1962 The Sword in Anglo-Saxon England

Dekker, T. 1609 The Guls Horn-Booke

Dover-Wilson, J. 1933 Paradoxes of Defence

Egan, P. 1812 Boxiana
– 1818-24 Boxiana
– 1845 Every Gentlman's Manual…

Elton (trans.) 1894 The Danish History of Saxo Grammaticus

England, Army 1887 Manual of Instruction for Single Stick Drill

Evans, Sir Ivor 1958 A Short History of English Literature, Pelican Books A72

Everyman's Library No. 489 1964 Ben Jonson, The Complete Plays

Firth, C. H. & Rait, R. S. 1911 Acts and Ordinances of the Interregnum (1642-1660) H.M.S.O.

Ford, Boris 1955 The Age of Shakespeare (Vol 2)

Fortesque, The Hon. J. W. 1899 History of the British Army

Gairdner and Brodie 1896 Letters and Papers (Vol. 15) of the reign of Henry VIII

Garrard, W. 1591 The Art of Warre

Godfrey, Capt. J. 1747 A Treatise upon the Science of Defence

Greg W. W. 1907 *Collections, Part 1*, The Malone Society

Grose, Francis 1775 *The Antiquarian Repertory*
– 1779 *The Antiquarian Repertory*
– 1780 *The Antiquarian Repertory*
– 1792 *The Antiquarian Repertory*
– 1786 *Military Antiquities Vol. 1*
– 1890 *The Antiquarian Reepertory*

Hardy, Sir Thomas Duffy 1873 *Syllabus (of Rymer's Foedora) Vol. II, 1377-1654*

H.M.S.O. 1960 *Acts of the Privy Council of England (1629 May-1630 May)*

Hunter, Rev. Joseph F. S. A. 1844 *The Great Rolls of the Pipe (II, III, IV, Henry II)*

Highland Officer (A) 1790 *Anti-Pugilism*

Holinshed, Raphael 1586-7 *Chronicles*

Holme, R. 1688 *The Academy of Armory Vol. I*

Holt, J. C. 1989 *Robin Hood*

Hope, Sir W. 1694 *The Sword-Man's Vademecum*
– 1707 *A New Short and Easy Method of Fencing*
– 1714 *Hope's New Method of Fencing*
– 1724 *A Vindication of the True Art of Self Defence*

Hutton, A. 1867 *Swordmanship and Bayonet Fencing*
– 1867 *The Cavalry Swordsman*
– 1882 *Bayonet Fencing and Sword practice*
– 1889 *Cold Steel*
– 1892 *Old Sword Play*
– 1895 *A Descriptive Account of 16th Century Sword Play*
– 1897 *Sword Fighting and Sword Play*
– 1898 *The Swordsman*
– 1898 *The Swordsman, A New and Cheaper Edition*
– 1901 *The Sword and the Centuries*

Jeayes, I. H. (ed.) 1905 *The Academy of Armory, Vol. 2*

Jewell, B. 1976 *Fairs and Revels*
– 1977 *Sports and Games*

Kellie, Sir T. 1627 *Pallas Armata*

Linsell, T. 1994 *Anglo-Saxon Mythology, Migration and Magic*

London Rifle Brigade 1895 *A Descriptive Account of Sword Play*

Lonnergan, D. 1771-2 *The Fencer's Guide*

Luders, A., Tomlins, Sir T. E., France, J., Taunton, W. E. & Raithby, J.
  1810-28 *The Statutes of the Realm*

Lupton, Daniel 1642 *A Warre-like treatise of the pike*

Macbane, D. 1728 *The Expert Swordsman's Companion*

Malet, Sir A. (trans.) 1860 *Roman de Rou*

Matthey, Col. Cyril 1898 *The Works of George Silver*

McCarthy, T. A. 1883 *Quarterstaff*

Mendoza D. 1789 *The Art of Boxing*
– 1815 *Memoirs of the Life of Daniel Mendoza*

Miller, Capt. J. 1738 *Treatise on the Backsword*

Musgrove Waite, John 1880 *Lessons in Sabre…*

Nef, J. U. 1963 *Western Civilisation Since the Renaissance*

Nicolas, Sir Harris (ed.) 1837 *Proceedings and Ordinances of the Privy Council (Vol. 6)*

Norman, A. V. B. and Pottinger, D. 1979 *English Weapons and Warfare, 449-1660*

Oakeshott, R. E. 1960 *The Archeology of Weapons*

Oliver, M. 1780 & 1781 *Fencing Familiarised*

Paylor, W. J. (ed.) 1936 *The Overburian Characters*, The Percy Reprints

Peecke, R 1626 *Three to One*

Picard, P. L. 1953 *Tales of the Norse Gods and Heroes*

The Publications of the Pipe Roll Society 1905

Pollock, W. H. 1890 *Fencing*

Quarrell, W. H. and Mare, M. (ed. & trans.) 1934 *London in 1710*

Riley, H. T. (trans.) 1859 *Munimenta Gildhallae Londoniensis*
– 1861 *Liber Albus*
– 1868 *Memorials of London and London Life* (1276-1419)

Rolfe 1935 *Loeb*, 195, M.A. 12. I

Ross, A. 1970 *The Pagan Celts*

Roworth, C. 1798 *Art of Defence with Broadsword and Sabre*

Sharp, Reginald R. D. C. L. 1901 *Calendar of Letters Book…*

Silver, George 1599 *Paradoxes of Defence*

Sinclair, G. 1800 *Cudgel Playing*

Shesgreen, S. (ed.) 1973 *Engravings by Hogarth*

Smith, Gregory 1907 *Addison's and Steele's 'Spectator'* Vol. 4 Oxford University Press

Stenton, F. M. 1963 *Anglo-Saxon England*

Stow, J. 1631 *Annales*

Strutt, J. 1810 *Sports and Pastimes of the People of England*

Swetnam, J. 1617 *The Schoole of the Noble and Worthy Science of Defence*

Taylor (trans.) 1837 *Chronicles of the Conquest* (Wace)

Thimm, Capt. Carl 1896 *Bibliography of Fence and Duelling*

Triphook, R. 1816 *Miscellanie Antiqua Anglicana*

Turner, Sir James 1673 *Pallas Armanta*

Van Muyden (trans.) 1902 *The Letters of Monsieur Cesar de Saussare*

Valdin 1729 *The Art of Fencing*

Vigfusson, Gudbrand and York Powell (ed. & trans.) 1905 *Origines Islandicae*

Waite, J. M. 1880 *Lessons in Sabre, Singlestick . . .*

Walker, D. 1840 *Defensive Exercises*

– 1840 *Wrestling*

Walpole, H. 1833 *Letters*, Vol. III, Second Edition

– 1757 (ed.) *A Journey into England*

Wheatley, H. B. (ed.) 1949 *The Diary of Samuel Pepys*

Wilde, Zachary 1711 *The English Master of Defence*

Williams, Sir R. 1590 *A Briefe Discourse of Warre*

Williams, J. (A. G.) 1639 *Pallas Armata*

Winn, R. G. A. 1890 *Boxing*

– 1890 *Broadsword and Single Stick*

Wright, T. 1857 *Dictionary of Obsolete and Provincial English*

Yonge (trans.) 1887 *The Roman History of Ammanius Marcellinus*, Bohn's Classical Library

Annon. 1625 *Mars, His Field*

BM. MSS. No. 34,192

Sloane MSS. No. 2530

Sloane MSS. No. 376

Queen Mary's Psalter

GLOSSARY of ancient words and spellings

When compilling a glossary of this kind it is difficult to know where to draw the line between what is obscure and what is obvious. In order to avoid difficulties for those readers who do not have English as their first language, it has been decided to include just about every deviation from modern English spelling used in the text.

able	enable	ar	are
abowdant	abundant	att	at
abyde	abide	avoyde	avoid
accoumpt	account	ayde	aid
admittet	admitted	beare	bear
affayers	affairs	begine	begin
agayne	again	belongethe	belong(s)
agaynste	against	belongith	belong(s)
agent	attacker	besyds	besides
agre	agree	betwyxte	between
agrement	agreement	backsworde	backsword
alowe	allow	basterd(e) sword	bastard sword
alowed	allowed	bodeley	bodily
als	alias	boke	book
alyens	aliens	bownd(e)	bound
achient	ancient	brabbling	clamorously/ noisily contesting
anciant	ancient		
ancyent	ancient	buckeler	buckler
anie	any	byend	bind
anny	any	Calleis	Calais (France)
apperteyneth	appertains	canot	cannot
apperteyninge	appertaining	carie	carry
appoyncte	appoint	chuse	choose
appoyncted	appointed	cnihtas	youth/retainer
approbation	approval	compasse	range/reach
approbrius	reproachful/ disgraceful	condiscended	condescended
		constitucions	constitutions

229

covenát	covenant	faythe	faith
convenaunte	covenant	fence	defence
couller	colour	folleth	follows
counninge	cunning	followeth	follows
courtain	curtain	four	for
courten	curtain	fower	four
cunstables	constables	Ffranc	France
d	penny/pennies	frefree	
daunger	danger	frends	friends
deceipte	deceit	fyend	find
ded	dead	fyne	fine
defendor	defender	fyve	five
defenc	defence	gennerally	generally
defense	defence	gev(e)	give
degre	degree	gevinge	giving
demaunded	demanded	grantith	grants
demaunds	demands	graunte	grant
desier/desyer	desire	grene	green
dew	due	Grenwich	Greenwich
discrecóns	discretions	grenwitche	Greenwich
disdeyninge	disdaining	graunte	grant
dismiste	dismissed	guyle	guile
disprayese	dispraise	hable	able
divers	diverse	halidome	holydom
dni	domni	hath(e)	has
doe	do	hear	here
donne	done	hed	head
doth	does	hinderanc	hinderance
drumes	drums	howers	hours
duetyes	duties	inp'mis	imprimus (first)
duetys	duties	judgem^t	judgement
dutyes	duties	juyn	June
ells	else	kepe	keep
endevor	endevour	kynd(e)	kind
estats	estates	lce	licence
euery/euy	every	lēē	letter
expyred	expired	lysence	licence
falcehod	falsehood	leste	least?
falshode	falsehood	lik wyes	likewise
fayled	failed	likewyese	likewise

lucar	lucre	pnts	points
ly	lie	poyncts	points
maiors	mayors	precense	presence
maister	master	priz	prize
mayster	master	profe	proof
mak	make	proffit	profit
maner	manner	promisse	promise
ma^tie	majesty	provoste	provost
matis	majesty's	provst	provost
mat^s	majesty's	pvost	provost
misdemenor	misdemeanour	pte	part
moneth	month	pties	parties
mony	money	publikely	publicity
moreouer	moreover	publique	public
mr/m^rs	maister(s)	quoth	quote
mste	most	quens	queen's
murtherer	murderer	raigne	reign
myles	miles	receved	received
mynde(d)	mind(ed)	recyve	receive
neade	need	rede	read
nether	neither	relme	realm
nic	Nicholas	requiering	requiring
nighe	nigh	ric	Richard
Nuegate	Newgate (London)	rome	room/ office/ position
nyneth	ninth		
obligacon	obligation	rueled	ruled
onc	once	ruelled	ruled
onely	only	ruills	rules
o^r	our	ryall	royal
ordinanceis	ordinances	s	shillings
ore	or	saie	say
othe	oath	sarvis	service
parson	person	sciense	science
pson	person	se	see
payne	pain	sealling	sealing
playeth	plays	sevall	several
playd	played	schole	school
plaid	played	scholer(s)	scholar(s)
plaide	played	sclander	slander

scyenc	science	viuat	vivat
shewe	show	VJ	VI (6)
shold	should	vp	up
sicknes	sickness	vpholde	uphold
sixte	sixth	vppon	upon
skore	score (20)	vnder	under
soch(e)	such	vnto	unto
soner	sooner	vs	us
soveraigne	sovereign	vsual	usual
spyte	spite	vtter	utter
standeth	stands	viuat	vivat
subiects	subjects	w^{ch}	which
subtile	subtle	weare	were
slue	slew	weikes	weeks
supreame	supreme	Willm/Wm	William
survince	overcome	Willm/Willyam	William
th	the	wone/wonne	won
thear	their	wrongede	wronged
thear	there	wth	with
theator	theatre	wthin	within
theatour	theatre	wthout	without
theire	there	wyes/wyse	wise
thefe	thief	wynn	win
theis	these	xcepte	except
thentent(e)	the intent	xpians	Christians
thre	three	y^e	the
tour	to our	yeald	yield
trueth	truth	yf	if
tryall	trial	yomen	yeomen
twentith	twentieth	you^r	your
twentye	twenty	yowe	you
tyme	time	yron	iron
unsaciable	insatiable	yt	that
ussher	usher	&c	etc.
vantage	advantage		
veneye[1]	a blow or wound		
veneye[2]	a hit or thrust in fencing		
venie(s)	see veneye [1] & [2]		
vidz	viz		

Additional Terms

agent - attacker

ap. - (derived from map) – son of

backsword/backsworde – single edged broadsword

bastard/basterd/basterde sword – a sword between the broadsword and the two hand sword in size.

bucklers/targets – It has become a matter of convenience to define a buckler as a small round shield held by a single grip, and a target as a large shield (in a variety of shapes) with two grips. It would be wise though to remember that this is strictly a convenience since contemporary book and manuscript illustrations show that the terms *buckler* and *target* were indifferently used by the writers of the time. For example, the book *Mars His Field*, 1625 (author unknown), contains illustrations of bucklers and targets showing both types having two grips. Equally, there are many illustrations in other sources depicting the buckler with a single grip.

commons/commonalty – the people

cricket pads – leg protectors

falchon/falchion – a type of sword. There are two distinct types of falchion, the first being that with an appearance similar to an Arabian scimitar. Indeed it has been argued that this type of weapon was introduced into Europe after the First Crusade of 1096 but it is more likely that it is European in origin and may have evolved from the Germanic seax (from which the Saxons took their name). The second type is cleaver like in appearance. An excellent example is the famous Conyers falchion. The name *falchion* derives from the Old French *fauchon* which in turn may be from the Latin *falx*, a scythe.

The **Conyers falchion** (see page 106) takes its name from Sir John Conyers who, according to legend, in 1063 used it to slay a poisonous monster that had killed and eaten many people. However, the decorations on the sword suggest that it dates from around 1260 and cannot therefore be the falchion referred to in the tale of Sir John Conyers. Nonetheless damage to, and wear and tear of, the blade strongly suggests that it was used in active service. It is a formidable weapon weighing 2lb 14oz (300gr) although originally, allowing for blade honing etc., it may have exceeded 3lb in weight. The length of the blade is just over 29 inches(74cm) though, since the tip is worn, it may originally have been an inch (2·54cm) or so longer. The total length of the weapon is just over 35 inches (89cm).

guls/gulls –
  (i) hangers-on; would be gallants. (From *The Age of Shakespeare*, vol.2, B. Ford, 1955).
  (ii) In modern English means credulous; naive.

hanger – type of sword. In the seventeenth and eighteenth centuries the term hanger referred to a light sabre. Originally, however, the term probably referred to a type of dagger, indeed some authorities believe that the name is a corruption of *khanjar*, Arabic for dagger. Hanger is also a Scottish name for a dagger and Holinshed (see p.14) clearly used the term hanger to mean dagger.

horn booke – sheet of paper displaying the alphabet, prayer, etc. mounted on wooden base and covered with a fine layer of horn.

husbandman – farmer

just length – perfect; ideal length

liber albus – white book

long (as in long Meg) – tall; tall Meg

long sword – two hand sword

patient agent – defender

play – fight; spar; compete

poiniard – type of dagger usually used with a rapier. Poiniards came in a variety of designs, often having a blade of square or triangular section. Some models had quillons which curved upwards more or less parallel with the blade (similar to the side tines of sais) enabling the user to trap his opponent's sword blade between the dagger's quillon and blade.

stand by (to) – to judge

stand at stick – to referee

tall (as in, *a verie tall man*) – brave; a very brave man. More familiar examples of tall in the context of courage are: Riding tall in the saddle (riding brave in the saddle) and tall ships of the line (brave ships of the line).

target – a type of shield.

INDEX

G

Gardant Fight, 98
George II, King of Great Britain, 81
Gewar, King of Norway, 78
Godfrey, Capt. John, 82, 83, 84
Goodwin/Goodwyne, John, 47, 49
Goths, 60
Gram, 61
Great Seal, 19, 29
Grenwich (Greenwich,London), 49, 50
Grene, Gregorie, 47, 49,
Grene, John, 44
Grene, Robert, 50
Gryffyn, Jeffrey, 19
Grymesby, William de, 14
Gunnar's Bill, 71

H

Hampton Court Palace (Surrey), 49, 50
Harris, John, 45, 47
Hastings, battle of, 72
Hartfordshire (Hertford,Hertfordshire), 46
Harvie/Harvye, Edward, 44, 45
Haye, Nicholas de la, 19
Hearne, Willyam, 30, 50,
Henry VI, King of England, 19
Henry VIII, King of England, 9, 18, 19, 20,
    25, 50, 62
Hockley-in-the-Hole (London), 52
Hogarth, William, 81
Holiwell (Holywell, London), 47
Horne, Roger, 45
Hood, Robin, 14, 79
Hother, 78
Hudson, Thomas, 19
Hunt, Willyam, 19, 28, 49, 50,
Hyfield, Hannah, 87, 88

I

Iceland, 55, 71
Ireland, 19, 26, 29, 36,

J

Jackson, John, 86
James of Castille (knight), 62
James I, King of England, 20, 25, 27
James IV, King of Scotland, 71, 72
Jonson, Ben, 40
Johnson, Tom, 86
Joyner, Willyam, 30, 44, 48, 49,

K

Kennard, Izake, 42, 46, 47, 49
Kings Head (tavern), 44
Kyng, Copin le, 14

L

Langford (blind fencing master), 61
Landknects, 72
Lausanne (Switzerland), 24
Leaden Hall (London), 49
Legge, John, 19
Leicester, Earl of, 18, 72
Letters Patent, 19, 21
London, 17, 21, 25, 28, 29, 30, 36, 39, 41
London, Lord Mayor of, 25
London prize ring rules, 84
London, Tower of, 72, 75, 76
Long Meg, 42, 62
Longe, Valentyn, 45, 47
Lord, Richard, 19
Low countries, 73

M

Man, Sir Horace, 15
Mary I, Queen of England, 20, 49, 50,
Mathew, William, 44, 45, 49
Mathews (stage-gladiator), 23
Mendoza, Daniel, 86, 87, 88
Medyna, Duke of, 68, 69
Miller, James, 40
Mjollnir, 13
Monopolies Act, 20
Morgan, William, 76
Mucklowe, George, 47
Mucklowe, Willyam, 27, 30, 44, 45, 46, 47,
    49
Murray, J.A., 11

N

Nailor/Naylor, Henry, 18, 30, 49
New Theatre, 23
Noble, Thomas, 44
Nuegate (Newgate, London), 48

O

Offa, Prince, 60
Office of Revels, the, 25
Olympics (ancient), 77
Ongentheow, King, 60
Otte, Willyam, 47

The Battle of Maldon
Text and Translation
Translated and edited by Bill Griffiths

The Battle of Maldon was fought between the men of Essex and the Vikings in AD 991. The action was captured in an Anglo-Saxon poem whose vividness and heroic spirit has fascinated readers and scholars for generations. *The Battle of Maldon* includes the source text; edited text; parallel literal translation; verse translation; a review of 103 books and articles.

This new edition has a helpful section about Old English verse – alliteration, English as an inflected language, auxiliary verbs, compounds.

£5·95   ISBN 0–9516209–0–8   96pp

Beowulf
Text and Translation
Translated by John Porter

The verse in which the story unfolds is, by common consent, the finest writing surviving in Old English, a text that all students of the language and many general readers will want to tackle in the original form. To aid understanding of the Old English, a literal word-by-word translation is printed opposite the edited text and provides a practical key to this Anglo-Saxon masterpiece.

£7·95   ISBN 0–9516209–2–4   192pp

Wordcraft
Concise English/Old English Dictionary and Thesaurus
Stephen Pollington

This book provides Old English equivalents to the commoner modern words in both dictionary and thesaurus formats. The Thesaurus presents vocabulary relevant to a wide range of individual topics in alphabetical lists, thus making it easily accessible to those with specific areas of interest. Each thematic listing is encoded for cross-reference from the Dictionary. The two sections will be of invaluable assistance to students of the language, as well as to those with either a general or a specific interest in the Anglo-Saxon period.

UK £9·95   ISBN 1–898281–02–5   256pp

Rudiments of Runelore
Stephen Pollington

The purpose of this book is to provide both a comprehensive introduction for those coming to the subject for the first time, and a handy and inexpensive reference work for those with some knowledge of the subject. The *Abecedarium Nordmannicum* and the English, Norwegian and Icelandic rune poems are included in their original and translated form. Also included is work on the three Brandon runic inscriptions and the Norfolk 'Tiw' runes.

UK £5·95   ISBN 1–898281–16–5   Illustrations   88pp

Looking for the Lost Gods of England
Kathleen Herbert

Kathleen Herbert sifts through the royal genealogies, charms, verse and other sources to find clues to the names and attributes of the Gods and Goddesses of the early English. The earliest account of English heathen practices reveals that they worshipped the Earth Mother and called her Nerthus. The tales, beliefs and traditions of that time are still with us and able to stir our minds and imaginations.

UK £4·95   ISBN 1–898281–04–1   64pp

A Handbook of Anglo-Saxon Food
Processing and Consumption
Ann Hagen

For the first time information from various sources has been brought together in order to build up a picture of how food was grown, conserved, prepared and eaten during the period from the beginning of the 5th century to the 11th century. Many people will find it fascinating for the views it gives of an important aspect of Anglo-Saxon life and culture. In addition to Anglo-Saxon England the Celtic west of Britain is also covered. There is an extensive index.

UK £8·95   ISBN 0–9516209–8–3   192pp

The English Warrior
from earliest times to 1066

Stephen Pollington

This important new work is not intended to be a bald listing of the battles and campaigns from the Anglo-Saxon Chronicle and other sources, but rather it is an attempt to get below the surface of Anglo-Saxon warriorhood and to investigate the rites, social attitudes, mentality and mythology of the warfare of those times.

The book is divided into three main sections which deal with warriorhood, weaponry and warfare respectively. The first covers the warrior's role in early English society, his rights and duties, the important rituals of feasting, gift-giving and duelling, and the local and national military organizations. The second part discusses the various weapons and items of military equipment which are known to have been in use during the period, often with a concise summary of the generally accepted typology for the many kinds of military hardware. In the third part, the social and legal nature of warfare is presented, as well as details of strategy and tactics, military buildings and earthworks, and the use of supply trains. Valuable appendices offer original translations of the three principal Old English military poems, the battles of *Maldon*, *Finnsburh* and *Brunanburh*.

The latest thinking from many disciplines is brought together in a unique and fascinating survey of the role of the military in Anglo-Saxon England. The author combines original translations from the Old English and Old Norse source documents with archaeological and linguistic evidence to present a comprehensive and wide-ranging treatment of the subject. Students of military history will find here a wealth of new insights into a neglected period of English history.

25cm x 17·6cm (10" x 6.5") with over 50 illustrations   UK £14·95 ISBN 1–898281–10–6 272pp

The Rebirth of England and English:
The Vision of William Barnes

Fr. Andrew Phillips

English history is patterned with spirits so bright that they broke through convention and saw another England. Such was the case of the Dorset poet, William Barnes (1801–86), priest, poet, teacher, self-taught polymath, linguist extraordinary and that rare thing – a man of vision. In this work the author looks at that vision, a vision at once of Religion, Nature, Art, Marriage, Society, Economics, Politics and Language. He writes: 'In search of authentic English roots and values, our post-industrial society may well have much to learn from Barnes'.

UK £9·95 ISBN 1–898281–17–3 160pp

Spellcraft
Old English Heroic Legends

Kathleen Herbert

The author has taken the skeletons of ancient Germanic legends about great kings, queens and heroes, and put flesh on them. Kathleen Herbert's extensive knowledge of the period is reflected in the wealth of detail she brings to these tales of adventure, passion, bloodshed and magic.

The book is in two parts. First are the stories that originate deep in the past, yet because they have not been hackneyed, they are still strange and enchanting. After that there is a selection of the source material, with information about where it can be found and some discussion about how it can be used.

UK £8·95 ISBN 0–9516209–9–1 292pp

We accept payment by cheque, Visa, Eurocard and Mastercard. For orders of less than £7 please add fifty pence for post and packing in the UK; £7–£14 add £1 p & p; over £14 add £1·50.

For a full list of publications see URLs: http://www.ftech.net/~regia/as-books.htm and http://www.anglo-saxon.demon.co.uk/asbooks/ or send a s.a.e. to:

Anglo-Saxon Books
Frithgarth, Thetford Forest Park, Hockwold-cum-Wilton, Norfolk IP26 4NQ
Tel/Fax: 01842 828430   e-mail: 100636.2512@compuserve.com

Most titles are available in North America from:
Paul & Company Publishers Consortium Inc.
c/o PCS Data Processing Inc., 360 West 31 St., New York, NY 10001
Tel: (212) 564-3730 ext. 264

Þa Engliscan Gesiðas

Þa Engliscan Gesiðas (The English Companions) is a historical and cultural society exclusively devoted to Anglo-Saxon history. Its aims are to bridge the gap between scholars and non-experts, and to bring together all those with an interest in the Anglo-Saxon period, its language, culture and traditions, so as to promote a wider interest in, and knowledge of all things Anglo-Saxon. The Fellowship publishes a journal, *Wiðowinde,* which helps members to keep in touch with current thinking on topics from art and archaeology to heathenism and Early English Christianity. The Fellowship enables like-minded people to keep in contact by publicising conferences, courses and meetings that might be of interest to its members. A correspondence course in Old English is also available.

For further details write to:
The Membership Secretary, Þa Engliscan Gesiðas
BM Box 4336, London, WC1N 3XX England.

Regia Anglorum

Regia Anglorum is a society that was founded to accurately re-create the life of the British people as it was around the time of the Norman Conquest. Our work has a strong educational slant and we consider authenticity to be of prime importance. We prefer, where possible, to work from archaeological materials and are extremely cautious regarding such things as the interpretation of styles depicted in manuscripts. Approximately twenty-five per cent of our membership, of over 500 people, are archaeologists or historians.

The Society has a large working Living History Exhibit, teaching and exhibiting more than twenty crafts in an authentic environment. We own a forty foot wooden ship replica of a type that would have been a common sight in Northern European waters around the turn of the first millennium AD. Battle re-enactment is another aspect of our activities, often involving 200 or more warriors.

For further information see URL: http://www.ftech.net/~regia or contact:
K. J. Siddorn, 9 Durleigh Close, Headley Park, Bristol BS13 7NQ, England
e-mail: regia@hrofi.demon.co.uk

West Stow Anglo-Saxon Village

An early Anglo-Saxon Settlement reconstructed on the site where it was excavated consisting of timber and thatch hall, houses and workshop. Open all year 10a.m.–4.15p.m. (except Yule). Free taped guides. Special provision for school parties. A teachers' resource pack is available. Costumed events are held at weekends, especially Easter Sunday and August Bank Holiday Monday. Craft courses are organised.

Details available from:
The Visitor Centre, West Stow Country Park
Icklingham Road, West Stow
Bury St Edmunds, Suffolk IP28 6HG
Tel: 01284 728718